After taking a degree in English at St Hugh's College, Oxford, Eileen MacKinlay taught mainly in secondary schools. She then lectured at Southlands College of Education, and is now Senior Lecturer in English at Newton Park College, Bath.

# The
# Shared
# Experience

John Milton, *aged ten*

# The
# Shared
# Experience

*writing and teaching:*
*towards a disciplined freedom in*
*the work of students and children*

## EILEEN MACKINLAY

*Newton Park College, Bath*

 Methuen Educational Ltd
LONDON · TORONTO · SYDNEY · WELLINGTON

*First published 1970*
*by Methuen Educational Ltd*
*11 New Fetter Lane, London EC4*
© *Eileen MacKinlay*

*Printed in Great Britain*
*by Cox & Wyman Ltd*
*Fakenham, Norfolk*

SBN 423 43970 7

Distributed in the USA
by Barnes & Noble Inc

*To my mother,
and to sixth forms and students
in gratitude for their friendship*

# Contents

*From your body's sap*
*in cold earth will spring*
*the brightest dandelion.*
*From your mind's furnace*
*spring the common flowers*
*of all men's minds.*

HILARY, *a student*


The *rules* of the IMAGINATION
are themselves the very powers
of growth and production.

COLERIDGE *Biographia Literaria*


Every one of these children
has a certain spark or gem of imagination.

DAVID, *a student,*
*speaking of his class of backward children*
*after his first year with them*

The first Light which shined in my
Infancy in its Primitive and Innocent
Clarity was totally ecclypsed: insomuch
that I was fain to learn all again. If you
ask me how it was ecclypsed? Truly by
the Customs and maners of Men, which
like Contrary Winds blew it out: by an
innumerable company of other Objects,
rude vulgar and Worthless Things that
like so many loads of Earth and Dung did
over whelm and Bury it: by the
Impetuous Torrent of Wrong Desires in
all others whom I saw or knew that
carried me away and alienated me from
it: by a Whole Sea of other Matters and
Concernments that Covered and Drowned
it: finaly by the Evil Influence of a Bad
Education that did not foster and cherish
it. All Men's thoughts and Words were
about other Matters; They all prized New
Things which I did not dream of. I was
a stranger and unacquainted with them;
I was little and reverenced their
Authority; I was weak, and easily guided
by their Example; Ambitious also, and
Desirous to approve my self unto them.
And finding no one Syllable in any mans
Mouth of those Things, by Degrees they
vanishd, My Thoughts, (as indeed what
is more fleeting then a Thought) were
blotted out. And at last all the Celestial
Great and Stable Treasures to which I
was born, as wholy forgotten, as if they
had never been.

THOMAS TRAHERNE *Centuries of Meditations*

# Preface

Almost all the writing by students that is collected here was done at a college in the west country. Our proportion of women to men is roughly three to one. Most of the students train for work in infant and junior schools. These facts are bound to be reflected in the character of the writing: in a town, for instance, there would have been different kinds of experience to write about.

In deciding which work to include, I have made my criterion not that the writing should be remarkable in any way, but that I should have learned from it.

For the students, teaching practices are times of vital growth. At the beginning they know almost nothing about the children. Seven weeks on their final practice is the longest time they have with their classes. A teaching practice often has to be a forcing-house. The class teachers are more fortunate; they are able to watch the 'very gradual ripening of the intellectual powers' that Keats believed to be the finest preparation for creative work.

Hilary writes on page 106 that 'the clear shadow of T. S. Eliot' can be seen over her poems. If anyone's clear shadow falls over this book, it is Coleridge's. In his account of imagination on page 1, usually referred to as his 'theory' of the imagination, he is describing what happens when he writes and when students and children write. Its validity is borne out time and time again by the writing published here.

The remark Turner is said to have made after hearing academicians talk – 'Rummy thing, painting', – is just as true of writing. But since the writer's thoughts take shape in words, perhaps words may be able to give a true account of the growth and the shaping: that is, the words of the writer, who should know what he is talking about. He will not pretend that he has explained the rumminess, the intractability of his medium. But something he has learned from immediate experience – like Keats's '. . . a regular stepping of the Imagination towards a Truth' – will root itself in your memory. You realize what it means when you see it happen.

> Dance there upon the shore;
> What need have you to care
> For wind or water's roar?
> And tumble out your hair
> That the salt drops have wet;
> Being young you have not known
> The fool's triumph, nor yet
> Love lost as soon as won,
> Nor the best labourer dead
> And all the sheaves to bind.
> What need have you to dread
> The monstrous crying of wind?  W. B. YEATS

The sea, in some contexts, can be an image of ephemeral things . . . The girl is innocent, and revelling in her youth. In the mother's womb, the child is surrounded with salt water. The girl has sea-spray in her hair. There is a connection between the two. . . . She dances in the wind and shakes the 'salt drops' of her youth from her hair; but the wind brings change, and perhaps she is dancing her last moments of innocence. This poem is rather mournful; but I think the dance for as long as it lasts is an image of eternity, because the girl, though dancing in this world, is not soiled by it. Out of men's minds fresh images are always being created. When a new image is made, it will have a brief moment of perfection like the girl on the sea shore, before it is changed by time.  JOY, *a student*

Like a cliff rising jaggedly from the sea and disappearing in a salty mist, it has square patches worn smooth – ledges for screaming gulls to balance their eggs on and for small rock flowers to grow.  CAROLYN, *a student*

> No more does the shell uprise no more
> for no more noise from the beautiful-like shell,
> silence for ever and ever more.
>
> But onemunts for ever on the sand.          (monuments)
>
> But one day soon they'll be no more
> for trampled on jumped on till they are no more
> But crumpled up bits.
>
> They used to house people
> But not our size of course
> But little sea urchings
> But they are no more.

Little sea urchings used to be
its inhabitunse
But now they are silent
Dead and no more.    CHILD'S POEM

In the first poem, Yeats is describing an experience – part of his
life and the child's: seen, felt, and absorbed into his thoughts. In
the paragraph that follows, Joy is attempting a criticism of his
poem. She is sharing Yeats's life, taking it into herself. In the next,
Carolyn is using images of things remembered from her childhood – experiences that she went on to share with children. The
elegiac poem was written by a boy of ten after listening to a
student's poem about a snail-shell. Like Yeats, the boy is communicating shared experience.

All these four pieces of writing are the work of what Coleridge
describes as 'secondary imagination'. In each mind whole experiences have had to be dissolved and fragmented in memories.
Imagination has shaped the fragments into a fresh whole.

All four depend for their existence also on 'primary imagination', the power of perception. Carolyn has noticed the square
patches worn smooth on a cliff face, where small rock flowers
grow. Yeats saw and remembered exactly the way Iseult Gonne
shook out her hair when she danced, the way wet hair falls and
tosses in the wind. Joy has opened her mind to the fullness and
freshness of Yeats's writing. The poem about the snail-shell has
quickened some experience already in the boy's mind, so that he is
able to re-create for himself the silence of the monuments 'for ever
on the sand'.

The students and the child may never become writers in the full
sense of the word. They are learning to write, and what they
write is ephemeral. They share with Yeats an ability to take in
experience through their senses and to feel sharply or intensely,
and the process by which memories dissolve and combine 'in the
twilight of imagination'. There is, of course, infinitely more in
Yeats's mind for the shaping imagination to handle; and the
shaping itself is a marvellous process compared with the simple
form it takes in the students' minds and the child's.

I should like to thank Cecily Nevill and Dietrich Hanff for our
talks on students' work in the schools; the College Librarian and
his staff for many kindnesses; and Pat Hattaway, my editor, Ann
Hughes and John Naylor for their sustaining encouragement and
help.                                        E.M.

# 1  Freshness of sensation

Everything we see is a proposal,
a possibility . . .

PAUL KLEE, *Diaries*

To find no contradiction in the union of old and new; to contemplate the
ANCIENT of days and all his works with feelings as fresh as if all had then
sprang forth at the first creative fiat . . . To carry on the feelings of childhood
into the powers of manhood; to combine the child's sense of wonder and
novelty with the appearances, which every day for perhaps forty years had
rendered familiar . . .

The Imagination then, I consider either as primary, or secondary. The
primary IMAGINATION I hold to be the living Power and prime Agent of all
human Perception, and as a repetition in the finite mind of the infinite I *am*.
The secondary Imagination . . . dissolves, diffuses, dissipates, in order to re-
create; or when this process is rendered impossible, yet still at all events it
struggles to idealize and to unify. It is essentially *vital*, even as all objects (*as*
objects) are essentially fixed and dead.

Fancy, on the contrary, has no other counters to play with, but fixities and
definites . . .

The poet . . . diffuses a tone and spirit of unity, that blends, and (as it were)
*fuses*, each into each, by that synthetic and magical power, to which we have
exclusively appropriated the name of imagination. This power, first put into
action by the will and understanding, and retained under their irremissive,
though gentle and unnoticed, controul . . . reveals itself in the balance or
reconciliation of opposites or discordant qualities: of sameness, with difference; of the general, with the concrete; the idea, with the image; the
individual, with the representative; the sense of novelty and freshness, with
old and familiar objects; a more than usual state of emotion, with more than
usual order; judgement ever awake and steady self-possession, with enthusiasm and feeling profound or vehement; and while it blends and har-
monizes the natural and the artificial, still subordinates art to nature; the
manner to the matter; and our admiration of the poet to our sympathy with
the poetry.  COLERIDGE, *Biographia Literaria*

## [ i ] The sympathetic imagination

This poem was written by one of the sixth form when I was teaching in a secondary school:

*Lois*

TOM O' BEDLAM
Poor Tom's King.
The rain and the bogs,
the purple owl's wing,
and the North wind's sobs;
the fields and the hills,
the frost and the warm,
where the marsh pool fills
and invites with its calm,
are all in my nightly care.
All mine as I dance stark
over the hills, and fields which stare,
and are full of daisies in the dark.
Why do they scream? Their hair in their hands,
their hands in their hair. I don't mind.
I couldn't care, for the manna of the land
is mine, and all that I find.
But the slime on my tongue,
frogs and rats from the water ditch,
and the bitter straw from the pied cow's dung
make me sick, in the ditch.
Belly-paining berries full of pips;
tiny birds' flesh full of little bones;
green corn, and the winter orange hips
I eat, until my lips are green foams.
The wind carves my stomach.
The armilla bites and buckles,
printing in pain, while I leap the hummock
and drill my eyes with broken knuckles,
weeping, screaming, lying in the hedges,
while the sour breeze carries
the warm salt drops to the warmer sedges,
like green woven cloth which stains and sullies.
I see all the stars at night;
every point; and I wipe my palm upon the sky
till all the sixpointed stars alight
are put out with the darkness in my eye.
I have been cold so I had nowhere
to put my foot, my arm, my leg;
my nose, my hands all ravaged by the air.
No movement gave relief: nowhere to put my head.

O Bethlehem the staples are strong.
So are the fits which ease all strife
for all. Around me are the long
rows of men singing in the gutter of their life.
Much rather the green countryside
where I can see them dance
in the black times, when they and I slide
on the coaching roads where travellers chance.
There is a maid who milks the cows,
and bends to the warm harvest task,
with her skirts girded up and half open her mouth.
I kneel in the hedge and watch her pass.
For this I am whipped and stocked
by mad fools who leave me
to the dancing fiend who worlds has rocked,
for all the little boys to see.
I who remember a mother's silky hand.
I who the moon commanded from the first.
I who plough a crooked furrow in the land.
I who am possessed, a vagabond accursed.

We had been reading *King Lear*. Lois's group had written essays
and read them to one another, and for their second piece of work
on the play I suggested a poem or some other kind of imaginative
writing. It was their first year in the sixth form.

Lois was sixteen. She had felt the experience of the Bedlam, and
Edgar's extraordinary sympathy for him, the sympathy of the
dramatist, actor, or poet who, Keats says, has no identity because
he is always 'filling some other Body'.

The countryside of the play, the imagery in Edgar's speeches,
and Lear's phrase 'loop'd and window'd raggedness' had worked
on her imagination, drawing in her own memories of fields after
dark and birds' flesh 'full of little bones'.

She had begun to understand the play. The part of her poem
beginning

> There is a maid who milks the cows,
> and bends to the warm harvest task,

makes a touchstone of sanity, so that the whole experience falls
into shape. It is a comment on the Fool's isolation, and King
Lear's. It is not only madmen who are cut off from the warm safety
of the girl absorbed in her harvest task, but also those who like
Cordelia and Edgar have to 'deal with grief alone', and those
whose sympathies are frozen: Regan, Goneril, Cornwall, Edmund.

B

I am sure that the others in the group had far more imaginative experience and a more lively vocabulary than they were using in their writing.

## [ ii ] A painter

Lois went from school to the Royal College of Art, and became a painter. Seven years later she wrote these notes for a catalogue of her work.

The paintings are about the strangeness of ordinary experience. To induce the spectator to see this, I use ordinary subject matter but try to treat it in an unfamiliar way (for example, unexpected treatment of scale). Close tones and saturated colour all contribute to this aim, but are also used to create particular sensations, such as time of day or quality of light.

All the factors that make my painting difficult to read at first glance are intended to surprise the viewer with a new aspect of the familiar.

A parallel can be seen in a common experience: that of finding the unfamiliar in what appears to be a familiar situation – a well known building seen from the other side of the hill, a close friend in a strange city. In the few seconds before shocked recognition, the landmark or person is seen with unprejudiced clarity.

'The strangeness of ordinary experience,' Coleridge says, is felt by the artist or the child who looks at things around him 'with feelings as fresh as if all had then sprang forth at the first creative fiat.' Hazlitt in his essay 'On Gusto' says that Titian's colouring 'leaves a sting behind it in the mind': both men have kept freshness of sensation intact from childhood.

Some of the writing collected in this book suggests that you are more likely to keep sensation fresh if you are a painter (Lois, Sally, Diana, Marie), a potter (Vic, Joy), or a sculptor (Alison). But all teachers need to be able to feel experience in this way. Some of them may have lost the power; but the infants, and most of the junior children they teach, will still have it. Some may never learn from the children, or may fail to recognize this power when they meet it. They may not know how to feed it through stories, poems, and 'ordinary' experience that is available every day. If there is a basic aim in the general course at Colleges of Education, it should be to crack open the students' fresh response to facts and things.

As they write, paint, or teach, they make discoveries that excited Wordsworth and Coleridge in their twenties. Lois's aim, 'to surprise the viewer with a new aspect of the familiar', is the same as Wordsworth's, 'to give the charm of novelty to the things of every day', and her instances of particular sensations given by time of day or quality of light correspond with what Coleridge noticed on the Quantocks: 'the sudden charm which accidents of light and shade, which moonlight or sunset, diffuse over a known and familiar landscape'.

Hilary in her account of finding cracked violins in a school cupboard and the imagery they suggested (page 105), and Diana saying that when she writes a poem it is because 'a visual experience suddenly connects with a thought' (page 12), are describing what is likely to happen when anyone, adult or child, writes as a whole person.

## [ iii ] Writing and painting

When I moved from a school to a College of Education, I was forced to think freshly. I was preparing students for examinations: there was still too little time for them to write in the ways they or I wanted, but there was more than the A Level syllabus had given us.

For main English I worked with a group of nine girls in their second year. We were out of college for several weeks at a time; the course work was refreshed by our contact with teachers and children in the schools. Our set period was the eighteenth century. It would be hard to find writers more remote from the children these students were about to teach than Addison, Goldsmith, and Sheridan. Everyone in the group responded to Johnson, and to Pope in his Satires; but the first real turning point came when we read Swift, and along with him, Golding, and the next when we went on to Coleridge.

Afterwards we read some Chaucer. One of the general groups had written about paintings – first of Watteau, then of Goya. We ought to have looked at these marvellous opposites while we were reading Pope and Johnson. I suggested as reading for an essay on Chaucer the first two chapters of Sir Kenneth Clark's *Landscape into Art*, 'The Landscape of Symbol' and 'The Landscape of Fact'. We collected reproductions of late medieval paintings and sculptures, whether or not they were strictly contemporary with Chaucer: the ones I remember are the King Penguin books on *Misericordes* and *The Leaves of Southwell*; postcards of effigies in English village churches, from a shop in Monmouth; pictures of people riding or working in the fields, from the Duc de Berry's *Book of Hours*, and the Perugia fountain; a book of Breughel; a photograph of a smiling stone face from a grange near Vézelay; and the British Museum illustrations to the *Roman de la Rose*. The group were to choose any aspect of Chaucer they liked. Sally wrote on 'Painting versus Writing, with special reference to Chaucer's Art'. This is part of her essay:

### Sally

It is difficult to find an exact parallel in contemporary writing to what Chaucer did for medieval literature; but there is an example in painting. Picasso tried to capture more than one impression of a sitter in a portrait. To do this he flattened all surfaces and put front, side, and back alongside one another. It is as if one were looking at a statue from three points at the same time. In Cubism he tried to discover the three-dimensional geometry behind what he saw, and its relationship to flat surfaces. It was as different from the painting of his day as Chaucer's *Prologue* was from the writing of his contemporaries. Chaucer made the figures of medieval literature into men and women with human oddities. Like Picasso, he wanted to show different facets that revealed their personalities.

In doing this, he revealed a great deal about himself. Portraiture is not a literal method of transcription; it involves the artist to a point where it takes so much that he is exhausted with giving. To a painter the finished portrait looks like the sitter: the two are identified in his mind because one has been made by absorbing, digesting, and reconstructing the other. The likeness is apparent to him, if not to an observer: he paints what he sees, and this is coloured by what he feels about the subject. Picasso can use the same girl as his model on many occasions, and each time different facets of her character will emerge – but always with the basic impression of freshness and mournful youth, which are what Picasso sees in the girl. I enjoy the Miller because Chaucer does; other people may have found nothing to like in him. We can construct the writer from what he writes.

Chaucer's medium is realism spiced with humour. He makes people live by means of his details, colour notes, and images. Everything that contributes to life is there: voices, sounds, faces, clothes, and behaviour. The figures are near to us, and solid.

In general, medieval painters concentrated on spiritual values, and delighted in pattern. Mountains were symbols of the loneliness and the temptation Christ suffered in the wilderness, fantastical rhythmic shapes echoing the lines of Gothic architecture (for example in Giovanni di Paolo's *St John the Baptist Retiring to the Desert*). Painters found formulas to represent people. In the fifteenth century Van Eyck looked at everyday life with fresh eyes, but even he takes us into a world of silences where action is suspended and emotion subdued. His painting of the Arnolfini marriage is serenity taken as far as it can go; the minuteness of detail presupposes a leisured viewing; the characteristic emotion is contentment. It is nearing realism, but is not quite there.

The romantic conception is the antithesis of this objectivity. In his early poem, 'The Wanderings of Oisin', Yeats concentrated on heightened emotion and luxurious imagery: he writes of 'night's purple cup'; 'eyes like wings of kingfishers'; idealized people, 'each forehead like an obscure star'.

Watteau had reached this pure emotion through nostalgia. Later, Turner used light to capture it, and Van Gogh turbulence. 'Used' is the wrong word. These things emerged as characteristics of their work – which underlined emotion, and expressed the particular character it had taken in each of them. Chaucer combined the intensity and objectivity of Van Eyck and his contemporaries with a freer emotional response nearer to that of Rembrandt, or late eighteenth-century and Romantic painters.

There have been painters who broke these wide categories; and these, as far as I can find, are the only ones who can be called realists. Breughel was one, working in the sixteenth century. His interest was in people as they were; and although this interest went with a satirical approach to drunkenness and gluttony, he must have enjoyed watching and painting exactly what he saw, not what he imagined he saw. *La Fillette à L'Oiseau Mort* painted by Jan Mabuse in the early sixteenth century comes still nearer to Chaucer's realism. Mabuse is commenting as Chaucer does on the character of the child, but like Chaucer he leaves certain things for the observer to interpret. Chaucer says that the Prioress wears a brooch with 'Amor vincit omnia' engraved on it. One's first reaction is to think well of the Prioress; but the words admit of a secular interpretation. Similarly my first impression is that the Mabuse child looks brutal and insensitive; but then I am conscious of a second feeling that this look could stem from her shock and disappointment on meeting reality in the death of her bird. Mabuse is a psychologist, with paint as his medium. I am using 'psychologist' to mean someone who probes for reasons behind actions and feelings, and sees them as mirrors of human character. Accepting this definition, I find that it fits Chaucer, too – except for the word 'probe', which does not say enough. Chaucer found that people often had reasons that they tried to hide from others, and he says what he thinks of these; but all the time he keeps a humane balance of feeling towards the person he is describing. He accepts that people are weak and make mistakes – often half consciously, for their own ease and satisfaction; and he enjoys their 'of-the-fleshness'.

His Friar, who should have been helping the poor,

> . . . knew the tavernes wel in every toun,
> And everich hostiler and tappestere
> Bet than a lazar or a beggestere.

This pictorial impression of pride at work, keeping the Friar from the poor, will stay in the mind longer than a mere statement would. Chaucer gives the man's own attitude, letting the reader note it for himself. He sounds as though he is struck with amazement at the Wife of Bath's head-dresses, and is asserting a wonderful fact: 'I dorste swere they weyden ten pound'; but there is an undertone of mockery. Of the Summoner he says,

He wolde suffre for a quart of wyn
A good felawe to have his concubyn
A twelf month, and excuse hym atte fulle.

The tone is no harsher, but a comparison is drawn between the quart of wine and the twelve-month-long sin that he would absolve.

With scalled browes blake and piled berd.
Of his visage children were aferd.

There is nothing amusing about his appearance: if there had been, the children would have laughed and jeered at it. The freshness of childhood serves as a contrast to the lecherous man.

Every portrait painter would, I am sure, say that he was trying to portray something of what is behind the external features. A poet, a biographer, a dramatist, or a novelist is especially concerned with the problem of how to show the motives and the true self that lie behind the façade shown to the world. Chaucer was interested in these façades and in what they concealed – the Monk's love of hunting, the Prioress's vanity. A painter can catch only one mood. He can capture one expression; and if this is not the one with which the observer is familiar, it will not, for him, be a true representation. He would never capture the glance for which a lover would look, or the lover the expression that is familiar to a child. Chaucer has a more pliable medium, and so he can show more than one side of his characters by putting them in different situations and describing their relationships with different people. The Pardoner is first seen singing with the Summoner, and thinking himself rather a dandy. Then he is shown selling his false relics, making a fool of the country parson. All the pictures Chaucer gives are necessary for a full know-ledge of the Pardoner: seeing him singing with the Summoner, one would never imagine him as he looks in church, 'a noble ecclesiaste'. These portraits are not, like paintings, of a frozen moment in life, true for one moment of time but only half true in relation to the whole of that life. Matsys paints a money changer and his wife in their environment; but he can show only a small part of their lives, leaving out many interesting and significant details such as what they wear on Sundays, or what they have for breakfast.

Words convey more than a painting can. Chaucer uses many images, and these evoke emotional as well as visual responses. The Squire is passionately in love:

He sleep namoore than dooth a nyghtyngale.

The image of the nightingale carries us further than the fact that it doesn't sleep at night. It is a singing bird with a lovely and melodious song; this connects with the line,

Syngynge he was, or flotynge, al the day.

It is a woodland bird, and the feeling it invokes is associated with soft warm places, secret rustling trees and bushes, quiet waters bathed in moonlight. All this deepens the impression in the reader's mind.

The Wife of Bath's stockings were of 'fyn scarlet reed'. Their colour suggests her gaiety: she enjoys all the pleasures the world has to offer. The Miller is dressed incongruously in a white coat and blue hood. These are colours the Madonna usually wears in paintings: they may have been used deliberately here, to make the reader notice the contrast. Chaucer varies his methods and jolts our minds. His strong dashes of colour differ from those in paintings, in that they are connected with images. The Prioress had 'greye' eyes (the word 'grey' might, at the time, have meant blue): the image 'greye as glas' suggests that they are shining, and that her nature appears to be child-like and innocent. Looking into grey or blue glass would be like gazing into frozen water; and the serenity and stillness given by this experience are transferred to the Prioress, and become identified with her. But his 'fyr-reed cherubynnes face' is far from being a reflection of the Summoner's character: a Cherub's celestial presence is the direct opposite of his lustful, earthy nature. His red face and scabby black brows would suggest evil, and hell fire. Poets have often included yellow hair in their descriptions of feminine beauty. The Pardoner had hair as 'yellow as wex'. The milky yellow of wax, its smooth greasy texture of tallow, makes an unpleasant sensation.

How to embody vitality in a work of art has always been the artist's problem. It is so easy to miss the spark of life and movement. Rodin, like Chaucer, met this problem, and he overcame it by using anticipated movement in his sculptures. In his statue of St John the Baptist, for example, the arms are in mid-swing – an active position, not a passive one. It could not be held for long; it is part of a complex movement. By catching the middle phase of a movement, Rodin suggests the whole. Two movements are caught in one: the relaxation of a step being completed, and the tension of a step being made. Chaucer's way of solving this problem is to use lively details and images. The picture of a sow, brought into his description of the Miller, suggests the qualities that are most animal-like in his appetite and manners; the mention of a fox, suggesting his cunning, links with what Chaucer tells us of his underhand dealings when he buys grain. Chaucer gets down to the essentials of real country life; instead of sentimentalizing about rambling roses and sparrows in the eaves, he mentions pigs, foxes, and spades. The Plowman's 'fother' of dung touches off many associations; it captures the freshness and the not-so-freshness of the farm. Chaucer thinks of giving us the intimate, least known details, such as the breakfasting habits of the Franklin: 'Wel loved he by the morwe a sop in wyn.' Eccentricities of habit or manner show character more vividly than things that are common to every man. Instead of telling us that the Squire had curly hair, he says that it looked as if it had been pressed into curl; the suggestion is that the young man was vain enough to have curled his hair if it had not been curly by nature. That the Wife of Bath was 'gat-toothed' shows us what she would look like when she smiled and attracted five husbands in succession.

Portrait painting puts the emphasis on visual knowledge, while writing embraces many aspects of knowledge. Paint changes with the years; it can yellow and dim; so that it is sometimes hard for us to understand the character of the painter or the sitter. In reproductions the original colours may have been dulled or exaggerated. Chaucer's pictures do not lose their freshness to this extent, because the colours and images still call for a response from the emotions.

Embrouded was he, as it were a mede
Al ful of fresshe floures whyte and reede.

If the Squire had been shown in a painted portrait, the way in which his contemporaries saw his gay dress might have escaped us because we are too far from the fourteenth century to appreciate the foibles of its fashions. But we can still feel the freshness of the flowers and the exhilaration of childhood and youth that meadows or green fields invite (as Dr Johnson once found). Because we can conjure him up in these images, the young man is still alive for us; so that differences in manners and costume are more easily allowed for. Today someone looking at the portrait of Giovanna in Van Eyck's painting, whilst appreciating the purity of line and delicacy of feature, might feel a general air of remoteness; I doubt whether a real woman would enter his imagination as he looked at her. But when we read Chaucer's description, 'Hir nose tretys, hir eyen greye as glas', our picture of the Prioress, if we want to think her beautiful, is different from what a medieval painter would see in his mind's eye, because our standards of beauty are different. So we are able to imagine her as a real person.

Writing will weather time more easily than painting; and, value for value, will come through more intact, having lost little by the transit of years.

When I gave back the essay Sally and I discussed whether it was true that a painted portrait could record no more than a frozen moment; how far certain words have changed their meanings, however slightly, or like colours in a portrait lost a little of their freshness in the five hundred years since Chaucer used them – 'embrouded' and 'nyghtyngale', for instance; and whether in his description of the Miller's clothes he would have chosen blue and white for their incongruity – indeed, whether colour in the *Prologue* is ever symbolical. We looked at the blue and white clothes of the hay-makers in the June scene of the *Très Riches Heures* of the Duc de Berry, and at a man (a cook?) in Breughel's *Bauernhochzeit*, dressed in blue with a white apron. We needed more time to find out about the glass in medieval cathedrals and houses, and the colours 'blew', 'greye', and 'pers' in the *Prologue*.

Sally had not read *The Waning of the Middle Ages* before writing her essay. Johan Huizinga, in his chapters on 'Verbal and Plastic Expression Compared', takes the point of view opposite to hers. He argues that poetry 'formulating a concept anew or describing visual reality' will 'exhaust the whole treasury of the ineffable'; while painting, 'even when it professes no more than to render the outward appearance of things, preserves its mystery for all time to come'.

In search of parallels and contrasts to Chaucer, Sally threads her way from medieval painters to Picasso, basing her conclusions on particular instances instead of repeating impressive generalizations from art critics. The essay is of more use to her, as a student and as a teacher, than a safer, more limited study would have been. As she writes she is learning about the inadequacy of words: for example, 'probe' (page 7), and 'use' in the sentence, 'Turner used light to capture emotion, and Van Gogh used turbulence' (page 7).

When we first discussed her choice of subject, she said she had not been able to find anything like Chaucer's realism in the painting of his contemporaries. I suggested that the nearest parallel might be the work of the Limbourg brothers who were painting just after his death, or of Van Eyck, their younger contemporary. She said that this was not what she meant by the representation of reality; and gave the example of Picasso, which she went on to develop in her first paragraph. So the essay came out of an argument. She is thinking, not merely reflecting attitudes given at school or in her reading. The argument is her own, and it excites her.

Her vitality comes to meet Chaucer's. In response to his nightingale image, her sentence about the secret trees and quiet water suggests what depths of sleep the Squire and nightingale resist; and the fresh meadow in the image describing the Squire's gown makes her think of Dr Johnson rolling down a field, in Boswell's *Life*. She uses her observation of people:

'. . . a painter would never capture the glance for which a lover would look, or the lover the expression that is familiar to a child.'

A painting will flash on your eye in less time than it takes to read a paragraph of writing. It will provoke thoughts, just as words will evoke sharp or intense pictures of real things. Without the paintings to give points of comparison and a second and third dimension, Sally would not have been able to develop such an open or antennae-like response to the intelligence implicit everywhere in the rich, spirited writing of the *Prologue*.

## [ iv ] A reason for writing

*Diana*

A writer never seems to me to need a reason for writing. It is just an action taken to release a thought or feeling, or both of these. Why he writes is an impossible question to answer. Yet when I think of release, this gives some idea of why I write poetry.

The first thought that occurs to me is that it was strange to begin writing poems at the age of eighteen. Was I merely going through a phase, trying my hand at writing? Then I remember how much I wrote between the ages of six and twelve. I once started on a book that got as far as several thousand words.

Something made me stop writing. I was using another medium for release. My painting and modelling gave me more satisfaction, and I had no need to write.

Painting, though, is limited in what it can say; and when I was eighteen, two things happened. One was that I became aware of what I was painting, whereas before this painting had been a purely un-selfconscious action. I could no longer take personal or emotional subjects and express them in paint. For a while I stopped painting, and being in need of a form of release, began to write again. The second was that I discovered that I had more to say than could ever be expressed in paint; and the new medium was writing.

I feel that my poems fall into two kinds: those that describe emotions or situations; and those that are philosophical: these are my bad poems. When I write, it is either because a visual experience suddenly connects with a thought, or because an emotion creates visual images. An example of the second kind is 'I thought I saw a black spider' – one of the first poems I wrote. An example of a visual experience creating a thought is 'The Pool'. The pool made me think of the three depths of thought that can be reached either in yourself or in another person.

I am aware that similar images occur in many of the poems. They also occur in my paintings, and are meaningful to me, though I don't know why I use them. For example, prismatic colours, reflections in glass, whiteness, dust in the air, and things with depths and many facets: all these I associate with beauty. Metals, sharp outlines, blackness, and noise, I associate with ugliness.

The later poems, 'Geriatric Ward', for example, were more difficult to write, and are not satisfactory. I should like to write simply, and the nearest I have come to this may be in 'Old Man'. The old man is my grandfather; and the poem says all I wanted to say.

> THE POOL
> I look down at the pool
> and see only the surface,
> stretched like a green skin
> from bank to bank,
> and pierced by rushes
> like clusters of bayonets
> thrust from below.
> Nearby a beetle scrambles
> through the soupy scum,
> and duckweed floats
> like eyes of fat
> in lifeless gatherings.
>
> I look again,
> and the water beneath

is sprinkled with a confetti
of sunlight and shadows,
where stickleback swim in circles
among the weeds.
A huge golden carp
appears from the edge,
easing its way through the water
with an effortless pulsing
of fins, and glides
slowly under the bridge.

I gaze for a long time
at the water beneath the fish,
where the image of the trees
dips down into the depths
and disappears;
but all I can see is darkness.


## THE SPIDER

I thought I saw a black spider
on the white wall.
It suddenly appeared
as though it grew out of the whiteness,
where the pureness of the colour was stabbed
and cried a black tear
which did not fall
but spread its legs upon the surface,
untouchable in ugliness.
Change colour, spider!
Change to white;
and let me see your beauty
like creeping fever
walk on black, and poison it.
No pureness then, nor any fear;
and I can touch you, so you run.


## THE COWS

Who left the cows out on such a night?
When the sky is splintered with stars
and the grass frost-strangled,
each blade a living crystal
crushed by our feet.
Sound is cymbal-clear,
yet they do not listen.
They stand, placed by a child's hand
on wooden legs, immovable –
breath and blood encased in cold air.
waiting for the morning's warmth
to set them in motion.

## THE GERIATRIC WARD

Now I understand complete timelessness.
Here in this glass-house of existence,
days fall away in heart-beats
or slowly move from light to darkness,
stepping on each second
as the clock struggles in its task.
Life is a pattern of opening and closing doors,
and waves of sound,
which may be remembered or forgotten.
Thoughts revolve round blotting-paper imprints
of past memories, jumbled and fading.

Sleeping and waking are one;
day dreams, night dreams fly together;
feeling and thought divorce.
Pain is God.
'Now' is the ultimate.


## OLD MAN

What does he think
as he goes to bed,
his flat slippered feet
like lumps of lead
plodding the creaky stair?
Does he wish he was dead?
Or does he just stare
at the dark musty wall
and the dust-blown air,
and not think at all?


## A FREAK IN HOSPITAL

No more than a keel of bone
under the sheet;
one hand, visible, claws,
but cannot reach the cup,
rested where the blankets are raised
but no body is.
Head grins on the pillow
in a mass of slobber and string,
eyes staring.
Feed it!
Mouth barks at me,
and throws shouts like an angry monkey,
No, no, no, no!
When there's whiskey, it smiles.

He has a mother.
Sometimes she comes,

and calls him by name;
fills the pipe with tobacco,
and seems fond of him.

Diana was in one of my general English groups. Her main subject was design. I used to envy my colleague who taught her,
because as soon as you went into his painting room you wanted to
pick up a brush and work there.

The writing she showed me was strong enough to develop on
its own. I read it, and we sometimes talked about it. It is much
more difficult to meet students in this way now that colleges are
expanding. At first we had groups of nine or ten; now they are
sometimes twice the size and it is almost impossible to know
people as individuals.

Diana says that for her writing is a form of release. She is releasing some intense activity that presses out from her mind and
feelings. At eighteen she has become 'more aware', she has 'more
to say' than she could say in painting.

She describes how images enter the mind. A thing seen with
heightened awareness 'suddenly connects with a thought'. Rushes
pierce the skin of the pool and a beetle scrambles over it; underneath sticklebacks circle and the golden carp 'eases its way';
deeper still, the reflections of trees disintegrate. At some stage –
perhaps through the different speeds and patterns of movement at
three levels, and the tree forms darkening – she finds the visual
experience suggesting the idea of 'the three depths of thought that
can be reached in yourself or in another person'.[1]

She makes a distinction between this kind of image and the
images in 'The Spider'. The second kind have come from a
reservoir of images stored in her memory; to make them, things
seen or touched – a drop of ink, a tear, a spider – have connected
not so much with thoughts, as with emotions. These are the
images that release, that have become symbols for her, and keep
appearing when she paints or writes.

Her writing is a form of exploration, an attempt to understand
experiences through expressing and ordering them. The experience is being ordered as the poem shapes itself in words and

[1] Cf. Coleridge's notebook entry: 'The white Eddy-rose that blossom'd up
against the stream in the scollop, by fits and starts, obstinate in resurrection – It *is*
*the life* that we live.' *The Notebooks of Samuel Taylor Coleridge*, ed. Kathleen Coburn,
I, 495.

lines. A poem, because it is both a release and an ordering, expresses controlled vitality:

> Change colour, spider!
> Change to white;
> And let me see your beauty
> Like creeping fever
> Walk on black . . .

The last poem, 'A Freak in Hospital', reaches a point of balance; it goes further than the poem about the spider. The earlier poem releases the shock felt when 'pureness', 'poison', 'fear' come together. Diana feels that it is the more satisfying of the two: perhaps because it suggests, disturbs, then leaves you to find your balance. But the balance in the later poem is a difficult, delicate balancing of three people's reactions, none of them straightforward: the mother's unclear emotion,

> Sometimes she comes
> . . . and seems fond of him;

her own complex feelings; the patient's helpless anger and smiles. Distance is balanced with intimacy, compassion with revulsion, identity with nothingness. The point of balance comes without comment in the last line,

> fills the pipe with tobacco.

The poem has ordered and contained a strong emotion, which continues to disturb but has been brought into relationship with other feelings and with a familiar, practical action. If writing can order feeling, it is valuable to students: a form not of therapy but of control. The complementary experience is their study of work where emotion has been ordered superlatively well: the plays of Aeschylus and Sophocles for instance – even in translation, or the paintings of Cézanne.

A good many students between the ages of eighteen and twenty-one feel an impulse to express their heightened awareness and a need for control. In Hilary's case (pages 104–9), there was also the need for contact with writers who would support, or challenge, her own thoughts about the world she had grown up in. She learned from the control in their finished work as opposed to their material in its raw state.

She saw the dangers of 'using the medium self-indulgently' (page 105). It is easy to release your emotion in writing that will embarrass a reader, easy to strike false notes when complex words, in the very act of expressing thoughts or feelings, can change their nature. It takes time to learn that writing will come to reflect the character of the writer only after it has been schooled into plainness – a plainness and a discipline that in the opinion of Wordsworth and the practice of other writers and painters make imagination 'severe'. It is hardest of all to write simply.

## 2 The fire in the flint
### *writing by children and students*

. . . the fire i' the flint
Shows not till it be struck . . .

TIMON OF ATHENS

### [ i ] Children's writing

These three pieces of writing by children in Swindon schools were done for our mature students on their second and final practice. I asked each of the students if she would describe the experiences that led to the children's writing.

*Doreen*

One day there was
a warterfoll
We saw it when we were on
Holiday.
It was glittering in the
sun, It was like warter
sparcs.
all the sparcs. Hit the
rocs. and Bownced away
to make a river.     PAMELA

Pamela had come from a formal school into family grouping. Her environment had changed from streets of closely packed houses to a new housing estate with a view of the downs, trees, and fields. This had been six months ago.

She was a happy child, eager to write about her experiences. She didn't ask for spellings, but liked to surprise me with a complete piece of work. She often brought her mother into the classroom; and I felt that her family background was secure.

I took a group of seven year olds for a walk. Pamela was one of them. They poked about in puddles on the housing estate, and wondered how they were formed. The stream we crossed was running rapidly; a tree trunk made a dam over which the water fell.

At school, we investigated porous sand, gravel, garden soil, and clay; and decided that a puddle must have clay at the bottom. We talked about an alpine lake (from a coloured picture), and thought of other kinds of water: the sea, rivers, streams, glaciers, canals, and waterfalls. I read poems about water and stories like *The Cow that Fell in the Canal* by Phyllis Krasilovsky and *The Little River* by Ann Rand and Feodor Rojanovsky. In a movement lesson the children were raindrops – at first light and slow, then heavy and fast; spots in a thunderstorm; bouncing hail-stones; swirling mist.

Pamela wrote about the waterfall after we had left water for wind and flight. She worked in the library where it was quiet. Her poem was spontaneous: I had no idea that she was writing it.

Pamela was out with Doreen and the children when they saw the little waterfall made by the fallen tree. Then the indoor experiences in their minds' eyes widened to lakes, seas, oceans, glaciers, and great waterfalls. In the movement lesson they became forms of water – feeling its gentleness, roughness, speed, noise, and the light travelling over it. It took some time for these happenings to come together in Pamela's mind. Later, Doreen asked her whether she really had seen a waterfall when she was on holiday. She seemed to have a confused memory of having seen one 'at Yarmouth'. Doreen couldn't find out whether this had been the case, or whether the waterfall on the housing estate had been transformed in her imagination by the experiences that followed. Her poem had its origin in feeling: feeling that had been gathering through each of the group experiences and was 'collected' again 'in tranquillity', in the library. The tranquillity gave way to energy, that made her sit down and write.[1] Her verbs 'hit' and 'bounced' make the power of the waterfall, and her simile turns into active metaphor:

> it was like warter
> sparcs.
> all the sparcs. Hit the
> rocs. and Bownced away
> to make a river.

### Marjorie

> once there lived a narstee
> king he had a wife the
> wife had a baby the king

[1] Coleridge, *Notebooks*, 1, 787, August to September 1800: '...so poetry... recalling of passion in tranquillity...'
Wordsworth, Preface to the second edition of *Lyrical Ballads*, written in the same year: '...it takes its origin from emotion recollected in tranquillity...'

had his wife behedid wen
the babe was twenfive
she had her farth                    [she had her father
hand she was crand Qwen        hanged she was crowned Queen]
one day the qwen
cold in her made
made get me a cop ov tee the Qwen
siad good biy then of she
went a hop and a scip and
a Jump she went she sut
the door then she went
down stes as she went
down stes she san a son
lar lar doo doo doo dar
a cop then she went
to the cow oh moo
bee cwiat sed the made      MIGUEL

Miguel was half Spanish. His father was a doctor, his mother had been a
concert pianist. He was fond of dressing up and loved to act as conductor in
our percussion band. My practice went on to the end of January and he wrote
the story in March, when he was six years and one month. On several days he
had produced fragments of stories; for instance on February 1st he wrote:
'Once a pon a time there were three bears. One was a great huge bear . . .'
Here it ended. On March 7th as soon as he got to school he began to write his
story. The rest of the class went on to reading, then to number work, but
Miguel continued to write, never once asking for help. When he had finished
he read it to the others with tremendous relish while they drank their milk.

The average age of the children was five years four months. Some of the
stories I read them were acted afterwards. Their favourites were Grimm's
'The Fish Wife', the Polish tale of the Glass Mountain (from *Once Long Ago*, a
book of folk and fairy tales retold by Roger Lancelyn Green), 'The Goat and
the Little Kids' (from *Stories for Seven Year Olds*, by S. and S. Corrin), 'The
Sleeping Beauty', 'Jack and the Beanstalk', and my version of *The Hobbit*. The
class teacher had read them A. A. Milne's 'The King's Breakfast' before I came,
and this seems to have influenced Miguel's story: it must have been in his
mind for at least a month (unless he had heard it at home in the meantime).
She had also read them stories of Winnie the Pooh, who always has a song
ready; and this may be why the Queen's maid sings as she goes downstairs.

Marjorie and the class teacher were in touch with the imaginative life that went on in the children's minds; they made the
stories part of this. Miguel listened to stories every day. He has
'The King's Breakfast' fresh in his memory:

The King asked
The Queen, and
The Queen asked
The Dairymaid:

'Could we have some butter for
The Royal slice of bread?'
The Queen asked the Dairymaid,
The Dairymaid
Said, 'Certainly,
I'll go and tell
The Cow
Now
Before she goes to bed.'

He has overlaid this with his own words, 'a narstee king', 'a hop
and a scip and a Jump', and his own brisk action. He is enjoying
the dialogue and the movement.

*Edith*

The big Magnet can Pick up the scissors
and the littl magnet cUdnot Pick UP the
scissors. and the Littl magnet cudnot
pick UP the scissors. The biG magnet
can pick UP the conkers and the Littl      [The conkers were in a tin.]
magnet cudnot Pick Up the Pen. and
the Littl magnet cudnot Pick Up the Pen.
the big magnet cudnot Pick UP the Littl
magnet. and the Littl magnet. and
the Littl magnet cudnot Pick up the big magnet.    MALCOLM

It was a school rule that the top infants should write their news every day.
For the first three days of my practice, Malcolm copied out the same two
sentences with slight variations: 'In summer I will be eight. I am going to the
Junior School.' I spent some time with him discussing his family, the school,
the work we were involved in – trying to draw him out. I suggested that there
were a number of subjects that he could write about without having to repeat
himself, and said that I expected him to have at least half a page to show me
next time. He stood looking at me, open-mouthed. On the next two days he
wrote his half page. To avoid disappointing me, he had copied from the boy
next to him. I told him gently that I would rather have one sentence he had
thought out for himself than a page copied from someone else. His writing
reverted to its pattern of one or two stilted sentences.

    Watching him afterwards, I realized that I had been unfair to him. He was a
heavily built boy who dwarfed most of the other children; and because he was
so much older, I had been expecting too much from him. It became clear that
writing was an ordeal. His letters were badly formed and poorly spaced; his
writing sloped down from left to right. Irrespective of self-expression, he
found the mechanics of writing difficult. (I noticed a similar lack of co-
ordination in his movements; he distributed his weight unequally when he
walked, looking at times like an outsize toddler taking his first tentative
steps.) He couldn't be expected to express himself imaginatively when he had
to concentrate so hard on letter formation. I stopped referring to the content
of what he wrote, though I still prodded him to write more, as I felt he

needed the practice. I closed my eyes when he went back to copying from his neighbour.

By the fourth week, I had resigned myself; I should never see any free writing from Malcolm. But during the week he came up to me bubbling with excitement. He had been experimenting with the magnets on the interest table. He poured out the facts that he had discovered. When he paused for breath, I said that I should like to tell the Headmistress, who would be as interested as we were in the magnets; but didn't know whether I should be able to remember the details. He said he would write them down for me.

He wrote three-quarters of a page. He watched me eagerly as I read it through. I told him how delighted I was. A minute later he was back again, asking for a nice piece of paper. If he wrote it out again very carefully, would I put it up on the wall for everyone to see?

What he had written was a piece of factual reporting. As might be expected, composition, spelling, and punctuation were poor; there was repetition, and confusion of case letters. But the writing has to be seen in the context of what had gone before and what came afterwards. It was the first time that he had wanted to write, the first time that he had written with interest and enjoyment, and the first time he had produced more than two sentences out of his own head. It seemed to me to be an enormous leap forward.

I left his page up for three weeks. Some of the children were almost as pleased as he was himself; they recognized that for Malcolm it was a 'good' piece of work. It served as an inspiration to him: he would wander off and stand looking at it, before sitting down to write. His writing began to improve in both form and expression.

It is interesting that after this he took a similar leap forward in Number – triggered off by some pattern work, and a walk on which we took particular notice of shapes.

Malcolm had been able to write sentences 'out of his own head' because by making something happen – on his own, and over and over again, he had learned a series of facts. His sentences all have the same pattern: half about the big magnet and half about the small magnet, bringing them into relationship. He is like someone learning to walk; sometimes it helps him to stand on the same ground, repeating a phrase or a complete sentence, before he is ready to take the next step. He sounds like a chiff-chaff piping on one note, but there is this difference, that his steps go forward: at each step the sentence has a new object. He is using words to record his learning of facts and relationships.

His learning progress was – to him – stupendous. He had built on his experience with the magnets. After their first demonstration, he wanted to know what else they could, or could not, do. If Edith had not brought them in, he might still have been copying someone else's news; and if he had failed to respond to the magnets, she might have accepted his inability to write.

## [ ii ] Students' writing

The general English course is difficult to plan. All the students take it. It was some time before I felt that I was beginning to understand their needs. I learned by the slow and often daunting process of trial and error. Vic, a third-year student, describes this process in his teaching diary:

> There is a good deal to be said for making mistakes or doing things badly to begin with. Often this is enough to point to the better way. If it isn't, at least you have something to work on. Better to do something badly than not do it at all because you think you can't do it properly. Doing nothing develops nothing. Also, the effect of doing something is to alter, however slightly, your personality: your potential has been given the additional dimension of this experience. You cannot know what new awareness may develop as the result of this growth. The expression 'If you can't do it properly don't do it at all' seems to me to be a piece of arrogant nonsense.

I learned most on the days spent with students in the schools, and from comments they made in their diaries. This is a quick and on the whole an exhilarating way to learn.

I saw that unless I used what I learned and made it the basis of the general course, I should be of no use either to students or to children.

### Textures

Whatever man makes and makes it live
lives because of the life put into it.
A yard of Indian muslin is alive with Hindoo life.
And a Navajo woman, weaving her rug in the pattern of
    her dream
must run the pattern out in a little break at the end
so that her soul can come out, back to her.

But in the odd pattern, like snake-marks on the sand
it leaves its trail.     D. H. LAWRENCE

These descriptions were written by junior and secondary men and women in their second year, and a group of older women training for infant teaching.

We had collected a tongue fern, a clump of moss, the wing of a goldfinch, a cedar cone, a cat's skull, a sliver of white wood, an onion, and a piece of alabaster in its rough state. I asked the students to take three of these – or any things they liked to find for themselves – and describe the essential distinctive character of each (what Gerard Manley Hopkins called its *inscape*). Their writing was to be exact, and they were to use their fingers as well as their eyes. In an essay on clay work with children Vic used the phrase 'a kind of practised curiosity': this is what I hoped they would learn.

When I tap the empty coconut shell it has the ring of sun-baked clay; but when I cup it in my hand it has the rough primitive feel of wood sawn against the grain, except for the coarse fibres springing from it – they do not pierce like wood splinters, but thread between my fingers like string.

The skull echoes to my tap. My fingers explore the curves and cavities, now stripped of living flesh. I trace the seam, a delicate jig-saw fit. The teeth are bright white in yellow sockets, still firm and shining sharp.

The silky, feathery moss looks like millions of miniature ferns entwined. Fine stems grow vertically from the moss, on top of which sit slimy brown tufted seeds. The moss is fresh and young, and has a delicate pine-like smell.

The handful of moss is light as feathers, and silky green, with dull, dry ends in between the fronds. I blow, and the harmless spikes tremble; it has no resistance, it seems unreal.

A two-foot splinter of white wood, as light as balsa, but stronger. It looks like celery on one side, and is smooth; and there are feathers of wood on the other.

This solid block of ice, delicately patterned, freezes my palm, and dribbles cold water through my fingers. It takes away my warmth, and I take away its form and substance.

The feathers were dark grey and black, with pale grey tips. The brilliant yellow band across one half struck the darkness like a ray of sunshine. The down at the base of each feather was ice-blue and dull autumn brown. Dead maggots were tied up in these feathers. They were cream-coloured with black heads, smaller than pin-pricks, buried in the down.

This wing is soft and light like a dandelion head; but the individual feathers crack like frost-bitten grass, rasping like a full, ripe head of corn. It looks too fragile to support the weight of even a tiny bird, yet it is tough: not even the wind can wrench it from its body. If you try to part the feathers, they resist, then gradually separate, then come together again, like a sea-anemone when a shadow passes above it in the water. Each pinnule is barbed like some medieval instrument of torture.

I usually touch cobwebs by mistake. They suddenly cling. They feel dry and dusty, and disintegrate when I brush them off me.

The frothy suds glistening like mother-of-pearl on the water made intermittent explosions. I cupped my hand and held them, until they disappeared and left a little pool of milky water.

The thin onion skin: a loose first layer that crackles off and rips like paper.

The grasses roll in waves. They are buffeted and bashed down, until the rain revives them. They may be rough and reed-like to the touch, the sticky sap from their stems making your fingers tacky. Some cut into your skin. Their flowers can be blown, stroked, and pulled away from the stem, leaving a small brush-like head with notches and bristles.

Before the students wrote their descriptions I showed them some entries from a notebook Edward Thomas kept when he was eighteen. (He wrote on the fly-leaf: 'Field Notes'. Vol. V. February to April '96. at Surrey and Swindon.)

February 23 Tattered streamers of the water-grasses flap and rasp and rustle in the wind.
February 28 Waterflag sends up a sticky paper horn from among the dead old sheaths.
February 29 Splitting an old hollow dock stem, I break there by a delicate silken cocoon that had enclosed a spider not yet ready to emerge.
March 7 In Winter after rain the hedges are more beautiful than in summer . . . In the rain-crystal are mirrored the interlacing twigs which seem to surround them with a fine net.

After discussing their own writing we looked at some Hopkins and some Hardy:

. . . through the light/they (bluebells) come in falls of sky-colour washing the brows and slacks of the ground with vein-blue . . . if you draw your fingers through them they are lodged and struggle/with a shock of wet heads; the long stalks rub and click and flatten to a fan on one another . . . making a brittle rub and jostle like the noise of a hurdle strained by leaning against . . .

She went stealthily as a cat . . . gathering cuckoo-spittle on her skirts, cracking snails that were underfoot, staining her hands with thistle-milk and slug-slime, and rubbing off upon her naked arms sticky blights which, though snow-white on the apple-tree trunks, made madder marks on her skin . . .

Each of these pieces of writing records a particular person's way of seeing that leaves its trail like the Navajo woman's pattern in D. H. Lawrence's poem. People don't always respond with the same senses: in the first description of moss the inscape is made by its silky strands twined like ferns, its tufted seeds and pine-like smell; in the second by its dryness, weightlessness, and inertia.

Hopkins says in his note on bluebells that they baffle him with their inscape 'made to every sense'. As he draws his fingers through the flowers and stalks, he tries out images until he has re-created the bluebells in every facet of this inscape:

'some wind instrument with stops – a trombone perhaps'
'a staff with a simple crook'
'when more waved throughout, like the waves riding through a whip that is being smacked'.

In a sense, the special nature of onion skin or the structure of a skull will choose the words itself – though words sometimes come more easily when we speak than when we write. Gwyneth talked about the soap-suds (page 24) with her children, aged sixteen and fourteen:

'I said, "Let's listen," and we heard the bubbles pop. I asked for their help with words. After thinking, Gillian suggested "intermittent explosions". Richard had noticed the iridescence, but couldn't pin-point it in this particular word; eventually he thought of "mother-of-pearl". The "milky" look of the water was the impression left in my mind afterwards.'

As soon as the infants in Carolyn's class (page 62) picked up the hamster, instead of inarticulate 'oohs' and 'ahs', they began to use verbs that showed exactly how the fur, claws, or whiskers felt to their hands and cheeks. They were communicating direct experience, as Edward Thomas was when he caught the noises, textures, and movements of water-grasses in his verbs 'flap', 'rasp', and 'rustle': words that need to be spoken aloud.

After a week had gone by I asked the students to look at their writing again and try to concentrate their meaning in fewer words.

We saw that the least useful words were vague adjectives and limp parts of the verb 'to be', and that for the most part passive verbs, impersonal constructions, and abstract nouns sapped the life from their writing.

The real work was done by nouns naming essential things, many of them implying growth or movement (grain, shell, splinter, skull), useful comparisons and metaphors (like celery on one side, a delicate jig-saw fit), and above all the active verbs (ice dribbles cold water, onion skin crackles and rips).

These words are cells in which language grows: the Preface to the *New Oxford Dictionary* says that whereas the more learned words borrowed later have changed very little in meaning and scarcely at all in form, these native roots and early borrowings have developed many variations in form and ramifications of meaning. These are the words that have taken on most resonances from our experience and become symbols (grass, water, rain, wind, clay) or metaphors (sap, sharp, pierce, thread).

Things reveal themselves in action, through verbs:

> . . . tumbled over rim in roundy wells
> Stones ring.

The child's poem on pages 58 and 59 springs to life when she catches the hamster in movement:

> In the corner behind his wheel
> I saw him washing his face with his claws.

In her first poem she repeats the word 'nice' without feeling the need for verbs or precise adjectives; then she writes the second piece. Carolyn makes the comment in her teaching diary, 'This time she was involved in the experience. The description is actual and there is energy in the last line.'

Active participles make past verbs immediate (I saw him washing) or give nouns and adjectives the thrust of verbs (fibres springing from it, shining sharp). Passive participles involve you in an action and its results (sun-baked clay, broken bone). Active verbs (click and flatten) and nouns that are in essence verbs (a brittle rub and jostle) make you play out the action and be for that fraction of a minute bluebell stalks. The experience, however brief, refreshes you.

James Stephens once described in a broadcast talk how he sat down beside a leafy bush and tried to think himself into the bush; and a dancer in Ram Gopal's troupe thought himself into a peacock. Coleridge says that the instinct 'to pass out of our *self*' – most fully developed in actors, dancers, and writers – is characteristic of our human nature:

'The first lesson that innocent Childhood affords me, is – that it is an instinct of my Nature to pass out of myself, and to exist in the form of others.'[1]

A poet, Keats told Richard Woodhouse, is continually 'filling some other Body'. In a letter to Benjamin Bailey he described this as a 'Life of Sensations', and said that it was his particular way of 'hungering after Truth'. But Bailey believed that he could find out the truth by abstract reasoning. When Keats argued for the authenticity of the imagination, he was shocked. So Keats went on to tell him about the sparrow outside his window – 'I take part in

[1] Quoted from Notebook 47 by Kathleen Coburn in *Inquiring Spirit*, Routledge and Kegan Paul.

its existence and peck about the Gravel.' He knew that if he was to write he must keep his inner imaginative life in touch with the life outside him, always 'taking part in its existence' through sensation, which I take to mean through feeling and through the senses. Coleridge would have understood this straight away: in 'Dejection' he describes a state of mind in which abstruse research was stealing 'all the natural man' from his nature,

> . . . each visitation
> Suspends what nature gave me at my birth,
> My shaping spirit of Imagination.

This is the opposite of the life 'of Sensations' on which imagination depends for its nourishment. In his words to Bailey, 'a Life of Sensations rather than thoughts' Keats is using 'thoughts' not in its general sense but in the narrower sense of 'consecutive reasoning'. He says at the end of his letter that a complex mind – 'one that is imaginative and at the same time careful of its fruits' – would exist 'partly on Sensation, partly on thought'. Reason and imagination might each contain part of the other.

Hardy 'passing out of himself' into Tess is an example of the writer Keats describes, who is able to 'fill some other Body' through Sensation. What Tess suffers is sometimes conveyed through textures rather than emotions. In the passage about the apple orchard exact nouns – 'thistle-milk', 'cuckoo-spittle' – express more than their surface meanings. Secondary imagination is shaping Hardy's material through the words 'staining' and 'madder marks' that suggest two crucial experiences in Tess's life, the seduction and the murder. The sticky blights that rub off on her bare arms image what has happened to her; just as earlier, the few rotten apples on the stubbard-tree had become an image for her of the state of the earth, the 'blighted star'.[1] She is like the growing things she treads over; Hardy feels her fullness of life and her vulnerability in terms of fine natural texture. He asks at

---

[1] ''Tis because we be on a blighted star, and not a sound one, isn't it, Tess?'

(Tess was driving to Casterbridge with her brother Abraham in the small hours of the morning, when the mail-cart collided with their waggon and sent its shaft into the horse's breast.)

'Did you say the stars were worlds, Tess?'

'Yes.'

'All like ours?'

'I don't know; but I think so. They sometimes seem to be like the apples on our stubbard-tree. Most of them splendid and sound – a few blighted.'

the end of the first part why it was that 'such a coarse pattern' had been laid on it.

As I was looking with a second-year student at a poem she had written, I asked her if she thought she could make her writing less abstract. She said, 'But I want to write about abstract things.' Another said when she gave me her work, 'I've written two paragraphs about an apple: the one you asked for – pure description, the other with my own feelings.' In the first, where she had concentrated on the apple, her writing was much stronger; it spoke with greater wholeness and vitality.

Wei T'ai wrote in the eleventh century:

'Poetry presents the thing in order to convey the feeling. It should be precise about the thing and reticent about the feeling, for as soon as the mind connects with the thing, the feeling shows in the words; this is how poetry enters deeply into us.'[1]

## Animals

I asked a main English group to watch animals in the biology lab, and give in their writing at the end of a fortnight. This was in the middle term of their second year.

### RATS

The black and white rats move round the cage, ungainly and spread-eagled. They stand on their hind legs, grasping the bars with tiny naked hands and feet, their claws like minute well manicured nails. Their noses are raised, quivering in the air, as if their nostrils were their eyes. Each jaw shows small incisors, like a child's protruding teeth.

They drag their tails behind them, thick and fleshy. They hang like sloths from the top of the cage, scrabble from bar to bar, then huddle in a corner, watchful and evil.    LINDA

### MOUSE

At first the mouse sits in my hand, able only to exist; every hair and whisker vibrating and giving off glints of light and energy.

Then it begins to explore my sleeve. Its cold-flesh feet, so delicate in repose, move almost clumsily; and its progress is a sensitive blundering guided by the ceaselessly moving, finely twitching whiskers, and the hard vulnerable eyes of pink glass.    JILL

[1] Quoted by A. C. Graham in *Poems of the Late T'ang.*

SALAMANDER

The salamander lies along my hand, tail at my wrist, matt nose at my finger's second joint. His skin stretches tightly, and pulls across his backbone. Random spots of banana yellow erupt on his inky flesh, as though glossy paint had dripped on him.

His eyes, though gleaming more brightly than his skin, look nerveless. He seems cold and heavy.

Suddenly his length begins to writhe, and he noses between my fingers. His left hind leg paddles the air, while the right pushes him through the valley of my fingers to seek new boredom on the other hand.  DAVE

FISH

Some glide through the water; others dart, weaving in and out round their fellows like quicksilver, afraid to stay too long in one place. The tiny fish have startled expressions on their faces. Occasionally a tremor ripples through them, and ends in a flip of the tail. The larger fish squirm through the tremor with more fluid and deliberate movements, as if they were ridding themselves of an invisible skin, furtively; and afterwards they shiver with relief. Now they look earnest and beseeching.  DEIRDRE

AXOLOTL

Suspended in the fluid of this glass womb, it is a foetus expecting nothing. This solid amnion will not burst and give way to fresh growth: the axolotl must exist in bloated, aged infancy; its fat white flesh has no umbilical connection to an external life.

It is not allowed privacy. The maps of blue and pink life-lines transport its blood to transparent fins. It breathes to display the workings of crenated flushing gills which, as a final insult, are situated on the outside. Sloth has slid into its eyes.

The sun shines straight through the axolotl, as though its pale pulp was not there; as though it did not even exist.  PENNY

*Three-line poems*

The same group of students read translations of *haiku* in the *Penguin Book of Japanese Verse*, then wrote their own *haiku*, keeping the three lines but not the seventeen syllables of the Japanese form. Some of these hit hard enough the first time; others had to be whittled down, stripped of everything but essentials. We tried to see why three lines were right but four would not do, and what was wrong with the lines or complete poems that missed fire. Meaning, in each poem, had to be concentrated.

The sky is stained grey
and rain blown through the air makes
trees shine from the ground.    JILL

Between coal scars
in the valley,
children scream.
The rain,
sharp in its sting,
cannot speak.    BOB

Time grows solid
like a wall
between us,
but thoughts
chip seconds
off the night.    SUE

She stared at her reflection,
noticed
how the mirror grew older.    MARGARET

Through misty glass
the moon is a fierce fire
on heathy cliffs.    FIONA

Every time he spoke
a hawk flew out of his mouth
and clawed at my face.    PENNY

The evening sky
draws blood like a leach
through its darkening veins.    CHRISTOPHER

The poet makes sandals.
So we walk round Athens,
his work on our feet instead of in our hands.
From the taverns, Hadjidakis and Theodorakis
sing of a more eastern Helen.
But a Greek turns his face from a Turk in the street.    DAVE

   The group's experience of reading and writing *haiku* influenced
their criticism. One of them, Yvonne, wrote soon afterwards of
Yeats's 'The Four Ages of Man': '. . . a short, sharp poem. Yeats
sees man as being dominated in turn by body, heart, mind, and
soul. Each couplet is intense, and this almost stabbing down of
words makes a deep impression on me. Probably this comes from
my enjoyment of reading and writing *haiku*.'

*Firebird*

This writing by a group of first-year students grew out of material we had been collecting on the four elements (for work with children), and descriptions in two of the novels we had been discussing – Hardy's account of the burning of Bathsheba's ricks in *Far from the Madding Crowd* and Golding's of fire spreading on the island in *Lord of the Flies*.

We lit candles and talked about ways in which we could enjoy them with children, and listened to Stravinsky's *Firebird* Suite. Then we read Emily Dickinson's 'A Bird Came Down the Walk', Hopkins's notes on a peacock's tail, and Wallace Stevens's 'The Bird with the Coppery, Keen Claws':

. . . And then he drank a dew
From a convenient grass . . .

He glanced with rapid eyes
That hurried all around;
They looked like frightened beads, I thought;
He stirred his velvet head

Like one in danger, cautious;
I offered him a crumb,
And he unrolled his feathers
And rode him softer home

Than oars divide the ocean,
Too silver for a seam,
Or butterflies off banks of noon
Leap, plashless as they swim.

He shivers when he first rears it and then again at intervals and when this happens the rest blurs and the eyes start forward. – I have thought it looks like a tray or a green basket or fresh-cut willow hurdles set all over with Paradise fruits cut through – first through a beard of golden fibre & then through wet flesh greener than greengages or purpler than grapes – or say that the knife had caught a tatter or flag of the skin and laid it flat across the flesh – and then within all a sluggish corner drop of black or purple oil.

. . . Panache upon panache his tails deploy
Upward and outward in green-vented forms,
His tip a drop of water full of storms.

. . . He munches a dry shell while he exerts
His will, yet never ceases, perfect cock,
To flare, in the sun-pallor of his rock.

This preparation took two sessions in the second term. In the group there were girls who had come straight from school to college and two older men. They were an infant and junior group; some of them (including the two men) chose to take infants on their first practice at the end of the year. A few wrote both prose and verse descriptions, Rosemary for instance (page 34).

> . . . Her plumage shivered
> like thousands of flickering flames from a window.
> I was aware of a sudden swirling, a rush of warm air
> like hot breath on chilled hands,
> a blur of sparks.   NORMA

> . . . a lightning movement of her head, when every feather quivers like burning flames. The crown of feathery tendrils sways. Her eyes black diamonds, darting, piercing. Behind her a spray of floating red cascades like a waterfall.   JEAN

> He soars straight to the sun;
> dew his food, his power unknown.
> His breast a garden of colour.   JUDITH

> The firebird's body burns into the sky; flies through the air like the lick of a flame; rises from the ground a rainbow jet.   JANE

> The crackling heat of aromatic thorn
> dwindles to smouldering embers.
> But from the grey-veined ash
> a bird lifts on golden wings to the burnished-copper sky,
> its flight a wandering path of dancing flames.   PETER

> The tree stood by itself in a small glade, its white-hot branches forming a pyre.
> The crystal light sharpened my vision so that I saw clearly the perfection of the bird. Its golden eyes blazed and sparkled. Its beak was molten brass, its crest a fiery beacon. Flickering feathers made a ruff round its neck; and the great wings glowed, shielding the delicate structure of its body.
> Its tail fanned and threshed the flames, making fire-fly sparks surge upwards. Black armoured legs reached down into the furnace as its iron claws gripped the branches.   BOB

> Bead-like eyes like dew in the centre of a flower
> magnify the sunlight,
> glow, tingle with freshness.
> The body glistening wet
> a golden brown, a shiny black,

and the wings a
chain-mail of
linked feathers
sliding one against the other.
Filaments brush the ground.
And then the tail
amber, russet, crocus yellow,
vermilion, crimson, gold;
a crescent sunset
on the blackened sea.    GILLIAN

The beak was made of iron and ended in points as sharp as the points of
rapiers. When it closed, it sounded like the quick shutting of a pair of
shears . . . *and*

A flash of red and gold on the horizon.
Feathers of dripping fire;
its tail an arc of falling flame,
eyes fiery red rubies.
A feather dropped earthwards, a flaming red arrow.    ROSEMARY

Bob painted two wax resist pictures of firebirds, and a term
later Gillian brought us a bird she had made of stiff flame-coloured
ribbons, rose, orange, and crimson, to hang as a mobile. This reminded us that children will not always feel an impulse to express a
particular experience in writing: it might be more satisfying to
paint or build or weave something, or make it out of clay.

## [ iii ] The images of memory

Roots of some kind are as essential to the vitality of writing or
music as they are to the life of a plant or a person. Benjamin
Britten describes how as a young composer, 'muddled, fed up,
longing to be used', he came across a copy of Crabbe's poems in a
Los Angeles bookshop, and for the first time read 'Peter Grimes':
'I suddenly realized where I belonged and what I lacked, I had
become without roots.' Some of the most convincing writing
(particularly by older students and by children) is about known
places, people, and happenings. It is often shrewd, unsentimental,
moving, and richly comic. When I read it the question arises, are
the kinds of writing on pages 29 to 34 mainly perfunctory, im-

posed from outside, or do their roots go down into the writers' experience?

In this work I am trying to give the students an imaginary experience – of the firebird, or an opportunity for a direct experience – the animals, or asking them to find one of their own and concentrate it in a given form – *haiku*. There is a central point to radiate ideas and focus our attention: something we have in common for the time being. The students are not being asked to write out of nothing, and on something quite arbitrarily given. Each already has his own experience of fire, candles, birds, mice, rain, mirrors, sleeplessness. The given form or experience has only helped to draw out 'the images of memory' and set them 'flowing in on the impulses of immediate impression'.[1] Hopkins must have recorded the changes in the peacock's tail while their 'distinct, vivid spectrum'[2] was still upon his eyes. The feathers – their shapes, markings, and surfaces – set flowing in from his memory images of green baskets, fresh willow hurdles, slices of wet fruit, transparent skin, drops of dark oil. The flesh of his greengages and grapes made Gillian see her firebird's feathers 'glistening wet'; and then she thought of rings of chain-mail 'sliding one against the other'.

I asked the group whether they could remember where their words or images came from. Rosemary said that the 'dripping fire' of the bird's feathers went back to sparklers she had watched on bonfire night. Bob's firebird of iron and brass in the white-hot tree came from what he had seen many times in a blacksmith's forge. Peter, who had been a Commissioner of Police in Zambia, had in mind 'the fires that sweep through the African bush at the end of the dry season, when the undergrowth and grass have been shrivelled by the sun and wind . . . The flames surge into the branches until whole trees are blazing. Through the roaring of the fire can be heard the crackle of the vegetation, and burning fragments are whirled skywards. When they come to a road, the flames flare out to the other side and then, as if the tips are too heavy to support themselves, they recoil, leaving a flash of fire in mid-air. A tree that has fallen will lie with its trunk a smouldering column, the pattern of its branches clearly visible in the soft white powdery ash veined with black and grey streaks.'

Each child and student has experience that he can use in writing. Each needs experience and practice in writing, to make him want

[1,2] Coleridge, *Anima Poetae, Letters*.

D

to write. First someone must strike the flint. Later writing may
come of its own accord.

> *Poet.* A thing slipp'd idly from me.
> Our poesy is as a gum which oozes
> From whence 'tis nourish'd: the fire i' the flint
> Shows not till it be struck; our gentle flame
> Provokes itself, and, like the current, flies
> Each bound it chafes.

# 3 Magic and synthesis
## *stories*

Although I see it all in my mind's eye
There can be nothing solider till I die.
YEATS *The Double Vision of Michael Robartes*

. . . that synthetic and magical power . . .
COLERIDGE *Biographia Literaria*

## [ i ] Writing a story

Here are three stories written by second-year students taking infant and junior courses.

Writing stories, after descriptions and poems, brought them into a different relationship with their material.

The material was experience that they had re-created themselves. The process of shaping it, as their stories grew, involved them in problems of construction. The sets of problems varied from story to story but were similar enough to be recognized.

I wish I could have included more stories. Some students went on for a term or more, writing the story alongside other work. Groups of friends read and criticized one another's first attempts, and we discussed fresh ideas and difficulties.

The first story, Diana's, is longer than the others, so I have given it in outline except for the last dream sequence, which is intact.

### Diana

The difficulty in writing a story for children is that as adults we forget what it is like to think as a child, and are able to reconstruct the child's world only by observing children. We are on the outside, trying to get in.

My experience of children is limited, and my experience of writing even more limited; but at twenty, perhaps, I am not so very far from being a child myself; and to write from my own experience as a child seems to me to be the right way to approach the story.

I can remember clearly the fantasy world which I constructed in all kinds of play. I told endless stories to my brothers and friends, full of adventures and impossible happenings. Out of these early stories came two characters called Zassies and Kanties. Also a third called Jumping-Window-Man, who describes his abilities in his name. They became alive for myself and my brothers. Their adventures were related when we woke up too early for our parents, and crouched in a tent made of a sheet, weighted into position on the bedposts by the less popular stuffed animals.

The three little men have always been so real to me that it seemed natural to use them in a story. Zassies had his name changed to Zasya; and Kanties (a name that doesn't sound pleasing to my adult ears) became Taka – pronounced with a short 'a'. In process of time, I seemed to have lost the significance of Jumping-Window-Man, and so I didn't include him.

I think Stephen represents me as a child: I thought of myself as a boy – perhaps because I only had brothers. I would watch this boy, image of myself, play through many actions – like watching a film in which I played the main role. Often I would draw the stories in their sequences and make models of the characters.

Similarly, in the story of Zasya and Taka, I visualized every sequence, watching Stephen and the two men play their parts. I find that I can't write about anything that I can't see in my imagination. I have used memories of places as stepping-stones in the story. The mountain and valley are in Wales, where I have spent many climbing and walking holidays. The sea is also that of the North Wales coast. This was the most difficult part to write, for memories of familiar places crowded in too fast, and I had to re-write continually, and shorten my descriptions.

The story seems to me to fall into two distinct halves: the first written from direct experience, the second from imagination. When I lost Zasya and Taka in the sea, I also lost myself in the story. There was no need to wonder how it would end; and although I remember visualizing each part, I can't remember working it out. The desert, the hands, and the white goat happened as I wrote. I made no notes for any part of the story; and while the first half had to be re-written several times, the second was written straight off in its final form.

To the reader, the characters and ideas may appear simple and childish, and there may seem to be no reason why I thought of them. But looking at the story objectively, I realize to what extent I have explored one theme: that things are real when they exist in the imagination.

Thus the Mountain of Dreams contains nothing until someone dreams; yet there is always something there for those who wish to believe in it. Zasya and Taka became real to Stephen because he believed in them, and the strength of his belief is stressed by their appearing in his daytime existence. Imagination and reality cannot be divorced. Perhaps this is not a child's story, but a collection of musings on fantasy and reality.

## The Three Days and Nights

[Stephen met Zasya and Taka in a mountain cave, looking down on a valley and a river winding 'like snail's silk'.

When he woke up, they were there, in his room.

'You were standing in the Mountain of Dreams. That is where all the people who are dreamed about live. None of them really exist until someone dreams about them.'

Then they said goodbye, squeezed through the window, and jumped out. Looking down at the flower-bed, Stephen could see their foot-prints in the earth.

At school all he could think of was Zasya and Taka. Their yellow eyes seemed to stare at him from the pages of every book he looked at. When he lay in bed at night, he thought about them. It was raining. Their foot-prints would be washed away.

In his second dream, Zasya and Taka were carried out to sea. A fisherman 'with a leathery face tanned by the salt spray' scooped them out of the water 'among quivering, thrashing fish'. When he landed on a quiet beach, they ran into the trees. 'Each pulled up a leaf and tucked his head through it, bending it to fit his shoulders.' Soon they were walking along bare sand and they could no longer see the trees – 'only sand, and the sun like a great orange, always in front of them tauntingly'. Their leaf coats began to wither.

In his third dream, Stephen knew that they had been in the desert for a whole day and a whole night.]

The air was steaming with heat, and Zasya and Taka lay in the sand under their withered leaves. The piercing blue seemed to darken, and clouds gathered. They heard the rain burst out. Plup-plup-plup into the sand it went, until there were trickles of water running down their bodies.

'Like heaven,' said Zasya, his rain-splattered face smiling. He jumped up and pulled Taka to his feet.

'Look!'

They both looked; and there, all around, tiny green shoots were popping up out of the sand. Each was like a clenched fist of a baby, growing bigger and bigger until, everywhere, hands were spreading out and opening their palms to the rain.

Soon the sky cleared, the sun came out, and the hands stretched and flexed to feel its warmth. Zasya and Taka danced round with joy. They sat on the upturned palms and swung on the fingers. When they felt hungry, the hands offered them fruit and sweet-tasting water cupped in the palms. Afterwards they played games of catch, running between the hands, which reached out and tried to grasp them, sometimes gently swinging them upside down. Then they each lay on a palm with their heads on the curled fingers.

When they woke, there was no sand – only knee-high bushes, trees and grass. All the hands had disappeared except for the two they had been sleeping on. A black dog wandered out from the bushes, and lay down in front of them with his head on his paws. He didn't seem to be able to make up his mind whether he liked them or not. After a while he raised his head slowly.

'You've got cat's eyes,' he said suspiciously; and with that he walked away.

They wandered through the grass, and dressed themselves in fresh leaves. After they had walked for half an hour, they met a goat. He was a beautiful creature with a silky white coat and blue eyes, and taller than any goat you could imagine. He seemed to be expecting them.

'At last,' he said in a soft voice. 'Now that you've found me, I'll take you home. Climb on my back, and hold tight.'

The goat knelt, and they climbed up: Zasya in front and Taka behind. Before they knew it, the goat was away through the grass, and they were streaking down a hill covered with heather.

'Yipee!' shouted Taka, bouncing about and holding tightly to Zasya. They clattered across rocks, and leapt streams, the goat running straight and never tiring. It began to snow, but he didn't stop; and Zasya and Taka pressed their faces into his silky hair so that the snow wouldn't get into their eyes. Across the bare hills he galloped, until he reached the mountains; then underneath a frozen waterfall he stopped.

'I must leave you here,' he said. 'Goodbye.'

They climbed down. 'Goodbye,' they shouted, 'and thank you.' But he was gone.

They stood for a moment by the waterfall, and though their bare feet were on the snow they were not cold.

'Which way?' Taka asked.

'We'll have to climb the hill to see,' said Zasya.

Taka stumbled and fell on his face in the snow, but got up laughing.

'Not far,' called Zasya encouragingly.

When they reached the top, they gasped. They could see miles down into a green valley; and there was Dream Mountain.

'Hurray!' they shouted: and they rushed down the hill through the gorse, yelping and laughing.

[The story goes back to Stephen 'who turned over and smiled in his sleep'.]

## Alison

### The Tydian Circle

I climbed down the cliff path from the caravan to the beach, trying to keep up with the boys. The hard spiky grass scratched my legs as I brushed through the clumps. The boys had slithered along the cattle trough and were waiting on the other side to tease me as I crossed. This was our short cut. 'You'll fall this time,' they yelled to me as I dithered along. But I made it, and joined them on the beach.

It was Martin's turn to be on at lurky, and he was already building a pile of sand as den. Dave was going to throw the ball, because he was good at that sort of thing; and the further the ball was thrown, the more time we had to hide. I paddled through the water to get to a rock that was out of reach when the tide was in, and climbed on to it. I could see Martin chasing down the beach after the ball. I lay flat against the rock, panting for breath, hoping that he hadn't heard me splashing through the water. As I lay there, I felt my foot touching some stones. I turned round to move them, so that I could lie flat.

They were piled in a triangular heap. They were smooth, and richly coloured. I sat and stared at them. They were not really out of the ordinary, but they fascinated me. Then I saw Martin searching for me, so I flattened myself on the rock again and forgot about the stones.

We played lurky all that morning. Tired and ready for lunch, we started back to the caravan. The wind was blustery. White foam was swirling into the cove. We were playing round the cattle trough, when I suddenly remembered the stones. I yelled to the others to carry on, and battled against the wind down the cliff. I had to wade up to my waist to get to the rock. The tide was coming in rapidly.

I climbed on to the rock. The stones were no longer in a pile, but arranged in a circle: with a large stone in the middle. An odd feeling came over me. Had I moved the stones? I must have done. It was the centre stone that fascinated me. It was smooth and curved. I leaned over to look more closely, and now, within the shadow made by my body, I could see a sapphire thread spiralling through the grey stone. I picked it up and stared at it. This would be the prize stone in my collection. I put it in my pocket and dashed back to show the others. But when I got back to the caravan, I didn't want to show it to anyone. I wanted to keep the stone a secret.

'Are there any more punnets?' I asked Mum as I washed my hands for lunch.

'Yes, I left one out for you this morning.'

'I can't see it.'

In the caravan we had a tiny trap-door to sweep rubbish through into a box below. Chris always swept my punnets into the box to annoy me. This time he sheepishly crawled under the caravan, and got it for me. I sorted out my collection, but decided that the stone I had found that morning was too good to go in any of the punnets – so I kept it with me all the time. I kept it hidden.

That night, when no one was looking, I slipped the stone under my pillow. I liked going to bed in the caravan. We had four bunks partitioned off from the grown ups.

For once, I didn't want to chat to the others. I lay thinking about the stone, but soon fell asleep.

It was beginning to get light, when I woke to hear a scratching noise underneath the caravan. I lay petrified; but I couldn't scream. The rattling was coming from the trap-door. I watched it, lying still. It was moving slowly. Pin-points of light shone through. They were green; silently they darted and leaped about. Then, as quickly as they had come, they went, flickering out through the trap-door. I lay down again. They had reminded me of the hands of a clock in the dark. I was not frightened now; only curious. I realized that this was the same curiosity as I had felt when I had seen the stones that morning; and even more, now, I wanted to keep it to myself.

I carried the stone about with me as my most valuable possession. It was not until three nights later that I remembered. I heard the scrabbling again, and the luminous green pin-points began to dart about the caravan. There were more of them this time. They gibbered to each other, and scrambled over the book-shelves and clothes-cupboard. Suddenly they moved into a cluster. In the dark they formed what looked like a globule of petrol, thick and glowing. Then one by one they broke away. I lay still, pretending to be asleep. I could tell they were coming nearer. Each touched my face, and went away. I saw them disappear through the trap-door, quietly replacing it.

I got up very early, slipped the stone in my pocket, and crept out. It was a misty Welsh morning but the sun was breaking through, and from the cliff-top I could see shimmers on the water. I felt as if I was above the clouds.

I walked along the beach to a craggy archway, a trough through the rocks leading to another cove. Something was compelling me to move. I stood between the two coves. I felt something push my foot. I looked down, and saw a minute figure.

I squatted on the beach. He was no bigger than my hand. He had a thin lithe body joined on to a pair of flat toeless feet, a round head with enormous green doleful eyes, and a dot of a mouth. His frizzy hair shot out in strands like wire. His fingers, long and pointed, waved like tentacles on the ends of spindly arms. He was dressed in what looked like a striped shirt. Though he reminded me of a caterpillar or a sea-creature, there was something vaguely human about him. He stared at me, and his eyes seemed to flash. He was trying to say something in a peculiar language, waving his arms as if he was angry. As I crouched there, he jumped on to me. I shuddered; but curiosity forced me to keep still. Then he climbed into my pocket. He was moving the stone about.

He came out with his hair ruffled and stood at the edge of the pocket, hauling at the stone. Gently, I helped him pull it out; now I had it in my hand.

I was convinced that he was real. He jumped off me. I wished that I could understand his language. He stood at my feet, holding his hands cupped in the air. I looked blank. He bent down, picked up a tiny piece of shingle off the beach, and cupped this fragment in his hands. Then he dropped it and pointed at me; then at the stone; then at my hands. At last I saw what he meant. I held the beautiful stone cupped in my hands.

He was saying to himself, 'Good! She's done it at last!'

Then he looked up. He seemed harassed and excited, but he bowed low. His spiky hair touched his flat feet.

I let him explain.

'We knew that you were in possession of the Wyoggle Stone. We saw you take it from the Tydian Circle several days ago.'

I must have looked dumbfounded.

He said, 'I am the leader of a race of people called the Tydwylliogs. Something terrible is happening to us. You must see for yourself.'

He climbed on to a rock, and pushed. Then I could see into the ten layers of rock. Inside each, lived a family. They looked very much alike, except that some wore shirts without stripes. They were all crying or moaning. I put my ear to the rock. I could hear a mother sobbing. 'No, no, please not my daughter. I have lost my husband and my son,' she mumbled between sobs. In a tiny room with shells for chairs and sea-weed for curtains, six children were huddled, crying and screaming, 'Where is our mother?' Somewhere else, a little figure was yelling and pulling at her spiky hair.

I turned to the leader. 'What is happening? What have I done?'

'Now don't upset yourself,' he said, patting my toes. 'I'll try to explain quickly. Years ago, our ancestors were given the Wyoggle Stone by the last of the Penralltog race as he lay dying. He said that as long as we kept the stone we should lead a happy life. But he added that if ever we should lose it, the people would begin to disappear. (That family of children have lost their father and their mother.) But the Penralltog assured us that if there was still one group of Tydwylliogs left, the people would be brought back on the return of the Wyoggle Stone.'

I saw what I had done by keeping the beautiful stone. By now I was sobbing, too. I handed the stone back to him. My tears had flattened his hair.

A troup of men carried in the Wyoggle Stone. Suddenly Tydwylliogs began to appear from nowhere. Families danced and sang, children laughed and squealed.

The leader spoke again. 'I thank you many, many times. Now our race will live happily and safely.'

He handed me a stone. I had never seen anything like it before. It was no bigger than my finger-nail. It looked blue; but from its pitted surface different colours flashed – mysterious greens and purples.

'It's beautiful,' I gasped. 'Thank you!'

'I hope you will remember us by it. We are allowed no contact with human beings, except in times of absolute necessity. But we shall be able to see you when you walk between the rocks or play on the beach. Smile to us, even if you cannot see us.'

Before I had time to speak, he was gone. The rock was as jagged and sea-weedy as it had always been.

I felt sad as I wandered back to the caravan.

I never told the boys, and they wondered why I smiled when I walked through the passage-way between the beaches.

I don't know how the idea for 'The Tydian Circle' first came to me.

The place is a village by the sea in North Wales, where until I was six we spent most of our summers in a caravan. Once I began to think about it, I remembered all the associations my family had with the village. The caravan, the path down to the beach, the cattle trough, the game of lurky, the collecting of strawberry punnets, the hole in the floor are all real to me; and because of this I can write about them.

I like to be able to visualize a picture in my mind that is so detailed that I can describe it. It is like seeing a painting or a photograph. When I first started writing, the story was a kaleidoscope of memories of the place and our holidays. I began to write before I had worked out a series of events leading to an ending. As ideas emerged, I had to put them down in note form to remember them. Then I worked from these notes. The more notes I collected, the more I could see the story as a whole: it grew into a succession of happenings with a particular emphasis on descriptive detail. Writing it involved linking these happenings.

I had intended to write the story in the third person, but I found myself reverting to the first person. I think this was because my brothers and I were so closely linked with the place that it was impossible for me to use the third person.

The idea of the Tydwylliogs came from a head I had made, very simply, from a lump of wood. The head and nose were of wire, the teeth were nails, and the eyes flat stones with a frame of chicken wire. Before writing about them, I found myself drawing Tydwylliogs in the margin; but it wasn't until after I had described them in the story that I saw the likeness to the head.

Compared with the second part of the story, about the imaginary people, the first part was tedious to write and took much longer. I was swamped by my thoughts. This part was too full of personal memories.

I ran into several other difficulties. I had to let the reader see the size of the Tydwylliogs in relation to the size of the girl so that I should be consistent in my descriptions, and had to find a way of making her understand their language. I also had to decide how long the whole action should take and how much time should elapse between incidents. At first the story ended abruptly with the return of the stone. But I didn't want the ending to be an entirely happy one, so I changed it several times. To have made all the Tydwylliogs die would have been too drastic: I thought that if the ones who had disappeared returned when the stone was given back, but that the girl was not allowed to see them again, this would give the feeling I wanted.

Many of the changes were made after reading the story aloud to other people, who found faults that I hadn't noticed. It was written and rewritten over a long period of time. Sometimes I found it easy to write; at other times I laboured over it. It helped a great deal to get objective opinions.

## Keith

### The Dragon of Hekla

Yak had lived in Iceland all his life. For eight years he had been with his father and mother on a small farm near the north coast. Then his father decided to sell the farm; he thought it was time Yak went to school. The family had to move to the capital city, Reykjavik.

Iceland is a strange country, very different from England. Most of the island is high and rugged; towns are few and far between. The mountains are volcanoes. Icelanders are very proud of them.

Yak had never been in a city before. Naturally it took him a little while to get used to the traffic, the people, and the rush of city life. He enjoyed school and found many friends there. But at times he felt sad, and longed to return to the mountains: to clamber over the rocks, slide along the lava, and throw stones into the craters. He had never seen a volcano erupt; but he had heard his grandmother tell of the time when one of them, Askja, had exploded, and the fire and lava had lit the sky all over Iceland.

His father knew why Yak was sad; he, too, missed his old farm and the fresh air life that went with it. So he promised Yak that on his tenth birthday they would drive out to Hekla, a volcano about eighty miles from the city; and there he could do just as he pleased.

They made an early start. The roads were rough and it was eleven o'clock by the time they reached the lower slopes of the volcano. His parents began to prepare a meal; but not even food could stop Yak at this moment. He ran off towards the mountain, jumping and singing as he went. He had never felt so happy before.

Half an hour later he got to the top. He had stopped for a few minutes on the way up, to look at the sea and the tiny islands spread out in the hazy distance. Now he stood on the rim of the crater. Inland he could see the white cones of other, higher volcanoes, and the glistening ice of the glaciers. Below him lay a sight that was mysterious rather than beautiful. He gazed into the black depths of the crater. How he wished something would stir down there, if it was only a puff of steam! Many times he had imagined that he could see the white smoke rising: then a few sparks of fire would shoot upwards, followed by a sound like the rumble of thunder; and the white-hot lava would pour out, flooding the sides of the volcano. 'How exciting it would be,' thought Yak, 'but I suppose I'll have to wait a long time before I see anything like that.'

He picked up some stones and threw them as far as he could into the middle of the crater. This was fun: he could watch them dive into the darkness, and hope that one day the volcano would grow angry and throw them back at him. He was just bending to pick up some more stones when he heard a tremendous rumble coming from the bottom of the crater. His heart leapt. Was the volcano about to erupt? He peered into the crater, waiting for the steam to appear – just to make sure that he had not been imagining the noise; then he was going to run like mad before the fireworks started. But it was not steam that emerged from the inky depths.

Yak stood petrified. A gigantic purple dragon was clawing its way out of the mouth of the volcano and up the sides of the crater. It reached the top and stood towering above him. Its neck made an ear-splitting creak as it lowered its head towards the quivering boy. Yak wanted to jump into the crater and escape; but he was paralysed with fright. The dragon opened his mouth and displayed his orange teeth and horrifying purple tongue. Yak thought his end had come: but instead a soft, sorrowful voice said,

'I suppose you've come to laugh at me, and throw stones to make me angry. You are all the same! If I were an ordinary dragon, I'd gobble you up while I had the chance; but I haven't the heart to do that kind of thing nowadays. Years ago I would have welcomed something fresh and juicy to eat. Those days are gone; I've turned into a tender-hearted dragon.'

The dragon sighed. He snivelled, and a teardrop the size of a boulder rolled from his red eyes. The spray from one of these tears caused Yak to overbalance and tumble head-first into the crater. In a flash the dragon swept him up on his wing and tossed him on to his back.

He was still upset. 'I'm sorry to have made such a fool of myself,' he said.

Yak felt as if he was on the top of a moving mountain as they slid down the crater walls. All he could do was to hold on to one of the dragon's spikes. He couldn't see anything. Then a sharp point of light appeared below. He found his eyes closing as the brilliance came rushing to meet him. The dragon stretched his enormous wings and began to fly (as gracefully as anything the size of a double-decker bus can fly) round and round in a circle. Yak opened his eyes; blinked; and blinked again. Now he could see a fiery glow with flames shooting upwards, shining on the walls of the cavern and turning it into a whirlpool of colour.

The dragon flew down. The light became blinding and the heat unbearable. Then the dragon changed direction and swooped into a smaller cave set into the cavern walls. It was cool, and dimly lit by a green light coming from the far end. The dragon knelt down, and Yak dropped off his back.

'I'm out of practice,' he said. 'This has been my home for eight million years or so – not very comfortable, I'm afraid.'

'Did you say – eight million years?' asked Yak.

'Of course I did,' said the dragon huffily.

'Then how old are dragons when they die?'

'Oh I see what you mean,' said the dragon more cheerfully. 'Whereas *you* die when you are old, we dragons never really grow old. We may lose a few scales here and there, but *dragons live for ever*. Your school teacher should have told you that.'

'I haven't been to school for very long,' said Yak timidly.

'I can see that I'll have to tell you everything,' said the dragon sympathetically. 'All the mountains in Iceland are ruled by Kjarval, the King of all Dragons. He lives in Askja, the highest volcano in the country, with hundreds of baby dragons who help him in his work. He used to appoint a dragon to every mountain. The dragon had to swear that he would make his volcano erupt at least once in a million years.'

'How can you make a volcano erupt?' asked Yak.

'All I have to do is to catch a cold. Then I crawl into the green chasm.' He pointed to the glow at the end of the cave. 'It leads down underneath the lava that you can see simmering at the bottom. Then I have to make myself sneeze. Fire comes out of my nostrils and lights the lava. Nowadays a dragon has to qualify in the General Certificate of Volcanics, a subject we learn in King Kjarval's College of Dragons. But even after all this training he can never hope to succeed unless he can sneeze. That's my trouble, you see: I've tried a hundred and one ways to catch a cold, but they've all failed. This is my last day as keeper of Hekla! Kjarval will banish me to a dead volcano. I wish *dragons* could die!'

He began to cry. Soon the cave was several inches deep with his tears. Yak jumped on to a ledge. He felt very sorry for the dragon but he couldn't think of anything he could do to help. Also he was scared. How could he get back to his parents?

He needn't have worried, because after a while the dragon stopped crying and said, 'Now I'll take you up again. I hope you didn't mind listening to my troubles. I had to tell someone, you know.'

'That's all right,' said Yak. He jumped on to the dragon's wing and scrambled up his neck. The dragon launched himself into the central cavern and climbed steadily to the top. Yak took a last look at the amazing scene around him. Then suddenly it disappeared. Now he could see the sky; and before long they had reached the top of the crater. He wished the dragon luck, and the dragon thanked him.

Yak tore down the mountain slopes. He couldn't wait to tell his mother and father what had happened. But although they listened patiently to the story of his adventures in the volcano, they didn't believe a word of it.

His mother looked worried. 'I think you need a good meal,' she said.

'What d'you think dragons eat?' asked Yak.

'Never you mind about dragons. Just drink up this soup,' his father told him sternly.

'But it's cold!'

'Put some pepper in it,' said his father. 'That'll warm it up.'

'Pepper . . . Ugh!' moaned Yak. He looked miserably at the green pepper-pot. 'Pepper . . .' he mumbled. He repeated the word several times; and each time his voice grew louder. Then he seized the pot and set off in the direction of Hekla. His legs ached, and his lungs felt as if they were about to burst; but he pressed on, and when he reached the top he fell exhausted on the ground.

After a while he heaved himself to his feet and hurled the pepper down into the crater.

The boy waited on the rim of the crater. He was waiting for a sound, a very special sound. He began to think that his plan had failed.

He had waited half an hour, and was about to give up hope, when he heard a faint noise coming from below. There it was again, louder this time. The dragon was sneezing. The boy jumped in the air. His idea had worked!

Night was falling, and his parents were ready to leave. Yak felt restless on his way back to the city. He knelt on the seat of the car, staring at Hekla, which grew smaller and smaller as they rumbled along the mountain road. He had failed after all. Tired and disappointed, he curled himself up in the corner of the seat and drifted off to sleep.

Within minutes he was awake. He found himself lying in a heap on the floor. The ground underneath the car was shaking violently. A deafening boom split the clear air. They stopped and looked back. Another explosion was followed by the dazzling brightness of white-hot lava pouring from the crater, and flames that illuminated the sky for miles around with a glow as powerful as a thousand sunsets. The boy gasped.

In the depths of the volcano the dragon was watching the eruption at its base. He had flown round the green cavern sneezing, spluttering, coughing, and chuckling; and now he was crying again; but these were tears of happiness, because Hekla was his for another million years – thanks to a boy and a pot of pepper.

'What a day!' murmured Yak. 'The things I've seen and done are so astonishing that I can hardly believe them myself. The trouble is that no one else will believe them, either!'

I had never tried to write a story before. When I began, all I knew was that I wanted it to be about magic.

My copy of the *Geographical Magazine* had arrived. It had a supplement on Iceland with pictures and a map, and as soon as I looked at them I knew that this would have to be the setting of my story. Volcanoes have always fascinated me. We had studied a cross section of one at school, and this gave me the idea of a cavern inside a mountain. I chose Hekla. I wanted there to be islands near it: they were clear in my imagination. I looked at the map and, sure enough, they were there.

I invented a name for the boy. Askja and Hekla, of course, came from the map. I found the name Kjarval, for the dragon king, in *Grettissaga*, which my tutor suggested I should read.

I wrote the story in my second year and read it to the children during my

teaching practice as part of the work we were doing on fire. The least satisfactory part was the last section, from Yak's parting with the dragon to the
eruption of the volcano. In my third year I was busy with special essays and
my final practice, so it wasn't until the summer that I was able to settle down
to re-writing the story. At first I didn't enjoy this work. I couldn't revive the
spirit in which I had written the first version. But I wanted to give the reader
a more convincing idea of time passing, and to make this last part more
dramatic. I brought in the dragon again because I felt that what followed
should be seen from his point of view as well as the boy's, and because I didn't
want him to be forgotten. Also I thought that after the excitement of Yak's
experience there should be a period of quiet, so that the climax – the eruption
of Hekla – should come as a violent contrast. So I made Yak fall asleep on the
way home instead of watching all the time for the sky to light up.

I am still doubtful about the first two paragraphs. Perhaps they sound too
much like a text-book. But I thought some children might not know what
kind of country Iceland is, and visualize a place like the North Pole. So I let
them stand.

## [ ii ] Controlling and shaping

'I like to be able to visualize a picture in my mind which is so detailed that I can describe it.'

'I find that I can't write about anything that I can't see in my
imagination.'

Alison and Diana spent most of their time on painting or sculp-
ture. What they saw in their mind's eyes needed to be turned into
shapes more solid than words. Alison, modelling the head from a
lump of wood, was making one of her characters before she had
thought of a story or a name for him; her drawings of Tydwylliogs
in the margin were probably a form of transition to the more
abstract medium. But the words themselves, because they name
things she has seen, handled, and known, make vigorous outlines
and strong colours in my mind:

'In the dark they formed what looked like a globule of petrol,
thick and glowing.'

'. . . within the shadow of my body, I could see a sapphire thread
spiralling through the grey stone.'

A writer must know people and things in this direct way if he is to
convince a reader. The verb 'spiralling' has a kind of startling

energy that suggests the strange power of the stone; Alison had been excited by the climbing interlacing movement held in spiral forms.

Keith's subject was geography, not design; but maps are visual shorthand for the landscape of a country. The islands near his volcano were 'clear in his imagination'.

To prepare for the stories, we talked about the places and people we remembered best. I said, 'Begin with what you know.' Diana remembered mountains in Wales with gorse growing on the foot-hills; the hands pushing up from the soil are fists of bracken. The Tydwylliogs' frizzy hair shooting out 'in wire-like strands' came partly from the 'hard spiky grass' on the path to the beach where Alison spent most of her first six summers, and partly from the wire she used for hair when she was making the head. Keith describes the glow from the volcano as being 'as powerful as a thousand sunsets'.

We read aloud parts of *The Weirdstone of Brisingamen*, in which Alan Garner uses his knowledge of Alderley Edge in Cheshire side by side with his reading of myths and folk-lore.

The two girls are closely involved with the experiences of the children in their stories. The characters in Stephen's dream are ones Diana invented in her childhood. Alison tried to be detached, but the place was so much part of her life that she had to write in the first person. Her child's adventures may reflect a fantasy of her own childhood, or her adult feelings about disasters that happen to numbers of families – like earthquakes, floods, or Hiroshima: when I read the two scenes in the rock, this is what they suggest.

Keith did not begin with the same kind of involvement. Instead of setting his story on the Cornish coast where he had grown up, he chose volcanoes. But as far back as he can remember, these have been real to him. The alterations he made show that as the volcano became more substantial and clear, his two characters grew more alive.

Most of his problems had to do with the mechanics of the story: how things were to happen; how to give the impression of time passing. There was no need to select and shorten. This may be because he was not writing from direct experience. The part that gave him most difficulty was the ending. This was the point where he wanted to involve his reader most completely, and make his time sequence most convincing; and he found, when he came to re-cast this whole sequence, that his first excitement had evaporated. Alison, too, had difficulty with her ending. She knew what she wanted but had to re-write these pages several times before she felt satisfied. Diana, on the other hand, says, 'There was no need to wonder how it would end.'

Keith enjoyed writing his first section about the volcano and the dragon. Both these had existed in his imagination before he thought of the story and, once he had decided on the dragon's temperament, they would behave in a predictable way. Also he was not having to cope with a flood of personal memories. So that this part was comparatively easy to write.

It seems to Diana that her story falls into two distinct sections: the first written from direct experience, the second from imagination. In the first, she says, '. . . memories of familiar places crowded in too fast, and I had to re-write continually.' The second part came easily and was written straight off in its final form. Alison says almost the same thing: 'Compared with the second part of the story, about the imaginary people, the first part was tedious to write, and took much longer. I was swamped by my own thoughts. This part was too full of personal memories.'

It seemed strange to Diana that the part from direct experience was harder to write, while the part 'from imagination' came effortlessly as the story seemed to take over and write itself: 'The desert, the hands, and the white goat happened as I wrote.' This is the most memorable part of her story; its pictures are like images in poems or dreams. The memories described in the first part were brought into her mind by her conscious desire to write the story. Her will had to act with her imagination, selecting and combining memories of the kind Alison describes as pouring in and swamping her. She had to struggle to 'unify' them and 're-create' them in the form of the story. Coleridge says that the shaping power 'dissolves, diffuses, dissipates in order to re-create . . . it struggles to idealize and to unify'; and 'It is first put into action by the will and understanding: and retained under their irremissive, though gentle and unnoticed controul.' In the second part of Diana's story the control was so unnoticeable that she couldn't remember having worked on this part. What she describes as 'imagined', in contrast to 'direct', experience had accumulated over a period of time, perhaps from childhood onwards; it was already 'dissolved, dissipated', and already re-created; and now it seemed to move into shape of its own momentum.

Alison felt that her direct memories were too rawly her own; it took time for them to change into the less intimate experience that a reader can share in prose. When Diana began to write her second part, the imagined experience had already been made into depersonalized images. Is this what Coleridge meant by the imagination's struggle 'to idealize' as well as to unify?

In the second part of the story the imagination had been shaping her sequence, working together with forms of the will and understanding that were unconscious rather than conscious, that is to say, it acted in a state between the normal waking imagination and the imagination in process of dreaming. In this state, it is a truly 'synthetic and magical' power.

# 4 Imagination and fact
## *teaching diaries,*
## *and children's writing*

... the *potential* works *in* them, even as the actual works
on them.

COLERIDGE *Biographia Literaria*

Plain Imagination and severe
... wilful fancy. ... busy power ...

WORDSWORTH *The Prelude*

## [ i ] Science and poetry

It was here on the summit of Ben Nevis during September, 1894, that he
received the impressions that led him eventually to design what Lord Ruther-
ford described as 'the most original apparatus in the whole history of physics':
the cloud chamber.

The hourly observations for which he was responsible began at 5 a.m. and
he described what he saw when there was a continuous sea of cloud below the
summit:

'The shadow of the Ben on the surface of the sea of cloud at first reached to
the western horizon; its upper edges came racing eastwards as the sun rose.
On the cloud surface beyond the shadow would then appear a glory, the
coloured rings incomplete and rather faint and diffuse. The most striking of
all were to be seen from the edge of the precipice overlooking the great
corrie when the observer's shadow ... was formed on a thin sheet or wisp of
cloud only a few feet below ... This greatly excited my interest, and made me
wish to imitate them in the laboratory.'

[On his return to Cambridge, C. T. R. Wilson began experiments 'to produce a cloud artificially by the expansion of moist air, with the aim of studying
experimentally the optics of the glory'.

He was 'immediately diverted' from this study by a discovery to do with the
process of condensation; but after many years of experimental work 'per-
formed with the utmost skill and the most remarkable patience', he produced

in 1911 a cloud chamber 'in which the tracks of atoms or of subatomic particles appear as thread-like trails of tiny water-drops'.]

This obituary from *The Times* shows the creative power of the primary imagination in a great physicist, and the immense vitality of his secondary imagination.

C. T. R. Wilson's account of the circumstances that led him to begin his research is a piece of factual writing. His aim is to describe precise conditions and happenings, not his response to them. Yet can a man in such circumstances write impersonally? The description of the glory might have come from a writer's notebook. Coleridge made a note on the glory after reading about it in the transactions of the Manchester Philosophical Society, and used it as an image in the poem 'Constancy to an Ideal Object'. On the 26th August, 1800, he wrote an account of changing movement, colour and light in the Cumberland hills, and asked a question that shows his interest in scientific explanations:

'Morning-six o'clock-Clouds in motion half down Skiddaw, capping & veiling Wanthwaite. No sun, no absolute gleam/but the mountains in & beyond Borrodale were bright & *washed* – ... All the crags that enbason the Derwent Water very dark-especially walla crag, the crag such a very gloomy purple, its treeage such a very black green ... N.B. What is it that makes the silent *bright* of the Morning vale so different from that other silence & bright gleams of late evening? Is it in the mind or is there any physical cause?'[1]

Their alert, distinct perception is reflected in the verbs, nouns, and adjectives both men use:

'clouds ... capping and veiling Wanthwaite'
'a thin sheet or wisp of cloud'
'the mountains were bright and *washed*'
'the coloured rings incomplete and rather faint and diffuse'.

C. T. R. Wilson is 'greatly excited' by what he sees: 'its upper edges came racing eastwards as the sun rose'. This is partly the scientist's excitement at the possibilities taking shape in his mind, partly exhilaration of the kind Coleridge feels when he catches sight of the clouds '*washed*' by fresh light. The two kinds of excitement are not separate; the one runs into the other as if there is no clear dividing line between science and poetry, factual and imaginative writing. Each kind has its own exactness.

[1] *Notebooks*, 1, 789.

Coleridge recognizes the authority of another kind of writing. In a later entry (1016) he wonders 'Whether or not the too great definiteness of Terms in any language may not consume too much of the vital & idea-creating force in distinct, clear, full made Images & so prevent originality-original thought as distinguished from positive thought —'. The words 'vital & idea-creating force' could apply equally well to the scientist's imagination; but when he speaks of this force being consumed by 'too great definiteness of Terms', it is clear that he is thinking of the imagination of a poet. In the essay quoted on pages 118 to 127, Sue writes of a certain kind of image in poetry: 'The abstraction behind its mask is sometimes unformed in the poet's mind.'

In contrast to the 'distinct' observations of C. T. R. Wilson and Coleridge, this poem, written by Marie in her second year, is an attempt to record a relationship with natural things, an isolated experience of fear and reassurance. At the time she felt that it was unformed but that she couldn't do anything more to it.

TWO TREES

Tonight I went down
into the black dip of the valley.
Tonight
the brook was a black band
with arrowheads against the sky.
Tonight the meadow was white.

I went through the gate,
my feet sank into the snow.
It was not cold
though the sky flaked my blind eyes
till they were hoary.
Feet followed furrows,
mealy, hushed, outsounded
by dark purple air to the ear.
In front only furrows
converging,
darkening.

Slowly ahead
two trees called
fear;
they called clearer;
greater the fear,
greater the pricking of purple air,
greater the ties to go on.

I stopped only when I felt
the grip of barbed wire,
the thorns.
Some kind of solace
to my searching,
to stand the stare
of two grey trees
leaden like silhouettes
against falling water,
urgent;
greater the fear
with the rush of the spring.

I asked perhaps
too soon
too much,
so like an image
I found a mirror.

Many trees spoke,
some black
some white.
I thought they made me choose between them.
But the black brook
brushed black to white
unheeded.

Nothing but strangeness,
fear, huge proportions.
My asking overwhelmed,
I turned to go –
Lost sight of two,
looked at four, five –
I returned running.

There was the brook;
there were two trees,
their roots covered
by a mass of white sculptures;
their trunks together twigged;
their upper limbs
reaching, grappling
eastwards, interwoven.
They were everything there,
everything that happened.
I walked away
slowly.

I looked down quite naturally,
and saw a long branch,
fragile and white

on white ground.
I picked it up:
it was mine.
How small my branch with the wood.

I looked back many times,
but there were always two
I must always remember,
knowing only –
I saw them;
they were there,
understanding;
an answer, answering again.
Just to understand one more day,
and then perhaps another.
I carried my staff out of the meadow.

Marie's words are 'exact' in their own way without defining so
precisely that the force of the images is consumed. The abstrac-
tions behind her images of grey trees 'leaden . . . against falling
water', and the brook brushing black to white, are no more full
made and distinct than those in certain Chinese paintings – I am
thinking of a poet on a mountain-side with pine trees, a waterfall,
a bird in the snow (in *L'Art de l'Extrême Orient*, René Grousset).
They work in my mind after I have read the poem.

Sir Kenneth Clark says in his book on Leonardo da Vinci: 'Although Leonardo's approach has become more scientific, he still
sees with the eye of a painter . . . A drawing of the Alps . . .
contains an elaborate note on the colour of mountain flowers
when seen through a great gulf of intervening air at a considerable
height.'

In the part of his treatise on painting about looking at walls
stained with damp, stones of uneven colour, or embers in the
fire, and seeing in them 'divine landscapes, adorned with mountains, ruins, rocks, woods', or 'battles and strange figures in
violent action', Leonardo is describing the same activity as Carolyn
in her account of the rock (page 57), and Vic in his note on the
children looking at clouds (page 78). 'In such walls the same
thing happens as in the sound of bells, in whose strokes you may
find every named word you can imagine . . .'. But the painter will
go on to reduce these imaginary shapes to 'their complete and
proper forms'; and for this, Leonardo tells him, he must study
as a scientist: '. . . be sure you know all the members of all the
things you wish to depict, both the members of animals and the

members of landscapes, that is to say, rocks, and plants and so forth.'

The eleven year olds Vic describes on page 79 lacked experience in 'thinking imaginatively about something that is usually looked on as a scientific phenomenon'. Leonardo's researches 'became fused with the texture of his imagination'. Ideally, in the growing mind of a child, the scientist's and the artist's ways of learning would be held in this kind of balance. He would enjoy animals, mountains, plants, clouds, and snow in both these ways.

## [ ii ] Infants

### Carolyn

This description of a rock was part of Carolyn's general English course work in her first year.

The infants she taught on her second practice wrote the poems on pages 58 and 59.

A ROCK

It is like a craggy mountain peak growing out of the earth, with gorges and chasms and a flat top.

The rock formation moves, rushing up and falling down like something growing – hundreds of dripping stalagmites of various ages, growing up close together. It is like a waterfall, and flashes of light catch the scales of salmon trying to leap the water.

Like a cliff rising jaggedly from the sea and disappearing in a salty mist, it has square patches worn smooth – ledges for screaming seagulls to lay their eggs on and for small rock flowers to grow.

It is the scaly coat of a Komodo dragon – a giant reptile with beady eyes. It grins as it sleeps . . . a contented grin as it stretches out in the sun.

It has spines like porcupine quills pushed backwards, and it sparkles like dewy grass growing in clumps.

It is like cigarette ash, and it glows like the skin of an antelope. In places, the putty-coloured dust clings, like pollen to a bee; rust flakes off; there are patches of green mould, and streaks of black and white marble, lying side by side with splinters of glass. The whole rock is rough and powdery, like bark.

TULIP
It has a funny green
Leaf at the bottom

of the stalk
and it is red and yellow
It looks like a soilger.

It is a pretty yellow
and orange in the middle
It is cold and smooth like hair
It could break
when the wind blows.　　KAREN

Choolips can be almost any coulours.　　BRUCE

PRIMULA
It looks lick a ladys hat
and the lefe looks lick a
chimmuny pot.　　VIVIAN

A PIECE OF WOOD
It is like a gun
it is ruff
it is blak brown　　BRUCE

CONE
It feels like a hedhog
It is sharp and brown
It grows on a fat tree
Baby birds wont sit on the pricks
It smels like an elephant.　　ADRIAN

SHELL
the shell is very very big
It looks like a hat that
keeps the sun out of your eyes
and if you turn it upside down
it looks like a pond.
it is very soft and has got lines
all over it. It looks like a
rain bo as well as a hat
The colour of it is orange and white.
If you turn it upside down
you could live in it
you could yoos it as a raft
or a boat
yoos it as a slide.　　KAREN

HAMSTER
Little Hammy Hamster

you are very nice,
I love your little wiscus
And your cage is nice.
I like Hammy's colour
He is brown like wood
Miss Downing's desk is brown
And his cage is bluw
Hes got a little nest
Where he keeps his food
Hes sleeping in a jam jar
In the corner behind his wheel
I saw him washing his face with his claws.     JACQUELINE

On her third and final practice Carolyn taught a class of twenty-eight six and seven year olds. These notes from her diary record the children's experience of writing, and suggest what else was happening in the classroom.

Monday 23rd January: I began the story of Jason and the Golden Fleece – half reading and half telling: ready for the work on wool, which I may be able to start tomorrow.

Tuesday 24th: We talked about sheep and places where the children had seen them. They were relieved to know that they didn't have to be killed to be sheared. They soon found out, as we handled the wool, that it was oily; and wanted to know why. Some of the girls began to sing 'Baa Baa Black sheep' while they were separating it into strands, and the rest joined in; then they sang 'Little Bo Peep', and some other rhymes.
  They wanted to know what happened to Jason and the dragon, so I went on with the story.

Friday 27th: (Talk about shells and the sea. Write a description of a shell.)
  Penny brought in catkins and forsythia, and we talked about these. I was surprised to find that a number of the children didn't know what catkins were called.
  They found talking about the shell difficult, and writing even more difficult. The shape and colour didn't interest them nearly as much as what had been inside the shell, or what might have been inside. Penny thought the shell looked like a hat, a hill for sliding on, and a Christmas tree: these were the only pieces of real observation that came from the class. I think I'll have to take this kind of work more slowly. They're not used to it; and though I could feel that the enthusiasm was there, I could also feel their 'I can't' attitude. They were serious about their 'I can'ts'. They need so much help with their vocabularies, which are very limited. And if they know which words they want to use, and I give them the spellings, they still can't find the link-words to make sentences for the 'proper' writing that will give them a sense of satisfaction and achievement.
  I must take in more things that we can talk about, appeal to their enthusiasm, and help them with key words like 'it is', 'there are', 'I am'. I'm

sure they should be helped to use their imaginations; but at the same time, they need the basic knowledge of how to go about writing.

We finished the story this afternoon. I played 'Puff, the Magic Dragon'. They decided that this was a different dragon from the one who guarded the fleece. Then I played Holst's 'Jupiter', which suggested a powerful, roaring dragon. Some of them felt that this was frightening, and preferred the music of 'Puff'.

Monday 30th: (Talk about the clothes they're wearing that are made of wool; discuss the colours, bringing in comparison: 'blue like the sky', 'blue like my eyes'.)

We talked about the colours of their clothes. The idea of enlarging on a colour seemed strange to them; and I found that their comparisons stemmed from things immediately around them. Sally said her jersey was the same colour as her teddy's eyes: I think she was the only one to qualify a colour. But they produced more writing than ever before. Penny and Elizabeth managed two pages each; there were repetitions, but they had made the effort to use words. This exercise took most of the morning. They were writing more factually than imaginatively, but I think this must be the way to begin. I will try again tomorrow. If they write about their families, this may give them confidence.

The dressing up clothes made the afternoon the most successful part of the day for four girls who staged a performance – more like a mime than a play. It was rather tiring for the ones who were watching, but I think they learned something about how to work together. The actors forgot themselves as soon as they put the clothes on.

We had an army painting the dragon model. Alan, David, and Elizabeth painted three splendid dragons to begin the frieze. Tomorrow we must devise some kind of background for these dragons to roam in. I have had suggestions of trees and ferns from David, but I must see what the others feel, and try to combine their ideas.

Wednesday 1st February: We looked at a crocus and a hyacinth this morning: we need to practise looking at plants. When it came to writing something on their own, the children seemed to be paralysed. After coaxing individuals, I managed to get them to begin; but with four of them, I had to fall back on writing a sentence at their dictation and getting them to copy it.

Steven prefers to write his news without asking me for help. It must be disheartening for him when he finds that I can't read a word of it.

Several children brought books about sheep or dragons, and we had impromptu reading sessions from these.

Thursday 2nd: (Yvonne making a shepherd, Karen a lamb. Valerie feeling a piece of lambskin, Susan spinning, Penny knitting, Elizabeth writing about the clothes we wear. Look at wool in carpets.)

Some of the children described what we did with the wool; then they wrote it out in their best hand-writing. It was good for their morale to see that they were able to produce a page of clear writing.

Tuesday 7th: This morning began, as usual, with their writing of news. Julie

needs help again: she has reverted to 'This is a mouse, a cat, a dog . . .' Most
of the others have some happening from the day before uppermost in their
minds. Yvonne needs a little pushing; if you leave her, she will write only one
line. Steven will copy a piece of news he's written before.

Wednesday 8th: (Talk about the sea, using the children's experience: waves,
sand, rocks. A. A. Milne's 'Sand between the Toes', Eleanor Farjeon's
'Waves'. They are to write whatever they please.)

After Play we talked for twenty minutes about the sea. Everyone had
something to offer. They enjoyed both poems. I was pleased with what they
wrote.

Penny produced two sides. Kim, left to herself, has always written, 'I went
to Valerie's house . . .', followed by a list of all the people she could think of.
Today she finished her poem without asking for suggestions:

> I am a wave and I am pushing
> the other waves and the water is blue
> and the water is all sorts of colours.
> It is blue and white and I am
> paddling and my mummy and daddy are paddling and
> even my grandpa is paddling.

Deborah, who writes very slowly and doesn't like making an effort, wrote

> I am a little little wave
> and I am very thin
> and I am blue
> and I am running on the sand.

The imagination that I was beginning to think was non-existent is there
somewhere! Heather doesn't usually exert herself, but she wrote a poem
with two unusually exact words for sound and movement: infants are usually
content with the verbs 'is' and 'was'.

> I am a little wave
> I am three different colours
> These are the colours I am
> Blue green and white
> I make a little rustling noise
> I am sliding onto the sand.

We talked about sea horses, because the class next door were learning
about them.

Wednesday 15th: Julie and Janet were bashing away at the xylophones,
clappers and bells; I could tell that they were trying to work out 'Three
Blind Mice'. One group were making a play; another had formed a knitting
and sewing circle, and were gossiping. The painters were seeing what
would happen if they mixed the primary colours.

They insist on painting their cats and dogs red, green, and purple. They
have no idea of realism at the moment; it doesn't interest them at all.

Tuesday 28th: (Talk and write about the hamster.)

There was someone watching the hamster all the time. The 'oohs' and 'ahs' changed to squeals when they held her; then they said her feet 'tickled' and her claws 'pricked'. They began writing about her in their books; and afterwards, for the first time, they wanted to make a neat copy. This went on into the afternoon. There could still be improvement – some were rushing at it and not taking care; but they finished what they had to do.

I should like their work to be more imaginative; but first they need more experience and practice, to make them want to write. On the whole the writing was factual and positive rather than expressive. This factual writing is valuable. But I would still like them to find their own words for describing things. At this stage, any word is exciting to them, and so they are pleased with what they write.

Thursday 2nd March: Penny and Karen have been measuring in paces. Their plans were haphazard, but it's difficult for them to detach themselves from the school at eye level and imagine how it looks from above. Geoffrey and his entourage are about to make their plan of the building. I am doubtful about the wisdom of giving these boys the freedom of the school; but perhaps the feeling of responsibility will do them good.

Today was one of those unexciting but satisfying days. I wanted to help the older children: I had noticed during the week that they were slipping behind in some activities, or hadn't quite mastered them. I think it was good for us all to take time to think over what we had done, and let it settle in our minds.

Friday 3rd: (Talk about cows. James Reeves's poem. Farm, grass, milk, udder; descriptive words for churn, dairy, sounds, sights; atmosphere words – coming from the children.)

After Play, we talked: this was the most interesting part of the day. I read the poem, showed them pictures, and told them about Austrian cows wearing bells. They suggested words to describe the cows: 'squelch', 'click-clock', and 'clip-clop'. Someone mentioned the cow's soft eyes, and the others laughed. So I made them all stare until their faces felt taut and hard, then got them to relax and smile. They went on for a few minutes, feeling their faces hard and soft.

Then I asked them to write a poem; and limited them to four lines. When they're not limited in this way they put down everything they can think of. I hoped they would choose the facts that interested them most.

Karen managed to get something of the rhythm that goes into the making of a poem, though hers was very simple:

> I like Jersey cows the best
> because the milk is nice
> the cows eat all day long
> and go to sleep at night.

David had thought of the word 'scrunch' for the sound of a cow's hooves. It was obvious that this was enough, as far as he was concerned, to give the atmosphere of cows. He wrote,

> 'Scrunch goes the cow.'

Roger wrote about cheese, though we hadn't mentioned it in our discussion.

They wanted to write out their poems again with the spelling right, and on better paper. They wanted to see them collected in a book. Even Deborah made a supreme effort, and not only wrote a poem but managed to copy it out in the time. Penny, who usually writes well, was in tears; so we wrote together. She had plenty of interesting ideas, but she was expecting too much of herself. Stephen surprised me with a piece of observation that was at the same time personal and universal:

> This cow it is a she
> and she makes a noise
> like you eating lettuces
> and she eats grass.

Monday 6th: Several children had been in the country over the weekend, studying cows. They gave me a good deal of information. Some brought pictures, books, anything they could find that had to do with cows. Janet asked me whether I knew that you could milk a rhinoceros if you wanted to.

Carolyn, training her class to write imaginatively, thought that even infants should be responsible for the wholeness of their work. She has added a note on spelling (after having taught for a year and a half):

At the end of my last practice we were going to make a class book of the children's poems. One child asked me if I could write hers out so that she could copy it with the 'proper spellings'. I did this for anyone who asked me to.

The age range in my present class is from six and a half to nine. Some children's work I hardly ever correct: they have enjoyed the experience of writing, and have found it an effort. With some, I only correct a word here and there that we've met before and that I think they will be able to remember in future. With others, I sometimes choose a word, give them a clue, and let them look up the spelling in the dictionary. It will be different every day and with different children. Now and again I insist that they choose one of their pieces of writing, and improve the spelling and hand-writing before we put up a display.

I didn't do this very often with the infants. They were just beginning; and they were so pleased that they could write at all that they were not interested in spelling, let alone concerned about it. But it is more important for the juniors. Society dictates that they spell certain words in certain ways, so that they may as well begin slowly and painlessly, now!

# [ iii ] Juniors

*Christine*

Christine made these notes for work with a class of nine and ten year olds on her last practice.

February 1st: The children must be sure of what I want from them. I will read them poems written by children of the same age, which I have duplicated for them. This will help to make them familiar with the shape of unrhymed verse, and encourage them to try their own hand at writing. It will, I hope, make them realize that what I am asking them to do is not an impossible feat. It will present them with familiar experiences.

First of all I want to ask them if they know what a poem is. We will read two poems by children about a dead tree root (from *The Excitement of Writing* by A. B. Clegg), then talk about the similarities and the differences between them, and ask why certain words have been used. The children will keep the sheets of poems.

At first they were surprised that the poems didn't rhyme; but they soon found that they were poems, all the same. Most of them preferred the second:

> 'Because it describes better.'
> 'Because it says more things about the root.'
> 'Because I like the last line.'

February 2nd: They are to write their own poems on a common subject, having first of all gleaned as many thoughts from one another as possible. We shall use the Devil's Claw shell to draw out images, adjectives, colours, and, eventually, poems. We shall share the experiences on the board, and try to gather enough material for everyone to write a poem. I want to see every child individually if possible. I don't want them to be inhibited by spelling and rhyme, so I shall tell them not to worry about spelling, though not to ignore it. I do want them to ignore *rhyme* at this stage.'

Before I began the lesson, the children took out the poetry sheets and were reading them – some whispering the words to themselves.

They were impressed by the shell, and there was hardly room on the board for all their ideas. We spent half an hour discussing images and adjectives, and recording them.

When we came to write the poems, most of the children were eager to begin, though a few couldn't think of a first line. I found that half an hour was only just long enough for them to write in; and then some of the slower ones hadn't finished.

THE SHELL AND ITS CREATURE
It is bumpy and lumpy like lumps in porridge,
It is spiky like a witch's long pointed nails,
or like a skeleton's hand,
it is like a crab with his claws reaching out for dinner
like a poisonous spider wondering who he will attack next.

It looks like a volcano spurting out moulton lava.
or like a mountain with snow melting beginning to show ground.
The bottom part looks like smooth delicate pink lips,
The animal that lived inside it was a delicate and fragile thing
It was slimy yet beautiful,
It was shaped like a frog,
yet much, much, much smaller,
It could not hear for it had no ears,
it could not smell for it had no nose,
The colour of it was a greenish yellow, and whenever you saw it
it gave you the creeps,
A shivering tickle goes up your spine
when his great blue eyes stare at you.
like two large blue marbles.    LINDA


The creature that lives inside this shell
is smooth and round.
It is yellow and white with long sharp claws,
and the eyes are a fiery red.
It spins silk like spider's webs,
and beams of bright sun.    EUNICE


It is like the skeleton of a hand,
It feels like a rugged stone.
It feels like a gnarled claw.
It feels so smooth
and looks like a fever on it.
It feels like lumpy hills
the top of a club with spikes.
like a cave with brown dirt on the side.
like a whiches finger wrinkled up.
the claws of a bear curved on the mouth of an unknown animal.
the points of a sobmerged rock in the sea
like cold freezing icicles.
Like overhanging clifts
and like a slimy worm laid on it awkwardly.
like spiral steps at one end.    STEVEN


If you touch it you will feel the claws attack.
But he is a marvellous Rugged and golden gleaming creature.
His enimes can never sight his golden wonders, for he too
can attack, you may not think that just an ordinary shell
can have fortunes.
You feel him walk over you like ghosts spreading his skeleton-like
hands all around.
However if an enime strike he opens wide his crevice another
victim.
From all round hes the wonder.    TIMOTHY

Instead of reading the children her poem about the snail shell, Christine used the Devil's Claw to draw out their own images, which seem to have freed the secondary, shaping imagination: in the second part of Linda's poem the process of imagining compels her creature out of the past into the present, seen more and more clearly.

The spiral steps, mountains with snow melting, poisonous spider, and creature shaped like a frog (one minute a reptile and the next almost human) are like places and people in J. R. R. Tolkien's Mordor and Rivendell. The accident of spelling in

> Like cold freezing icicles,
> like overhanging *clifts*

suggests 'The Ancient Mariner'; so do

> It is like the skeleton of a hand,
> . . . and looks like a fever on it,

and the creature whose eyes are 'a fiery red', who is coloured yellow and white like the Nightmare Life-in-Death,

> Her lips were red, her looks were free,
> Her locks were yellow as gold:
> Her skin was white as leprosy. . .

The kinship of these images used by the children with images in *The Lord of the Rings* and 'The Ancient Mariner' confirms what Professor Tolkien says in *Tree and Leaf*: that it may be better for children to read 'some things, especially fairy stories, that are beyond their measure rather than short of it'.

When Linda and Steven explore the surface of the shell, their images and their exact observation dove-tail. The shell and the child's mind produce two halves of an image. The child notices sharp points, a ridge, curved lines. These connect with things from his past experience – rocks, worms, a bear's claws. Steven is remembering the feel and fluid shape of a worm; and things he has seen clumsily arranged. His imagination pictures them in terms of the shell's structure:

> and like a slimy worm laid on it awkwardly
> the claws of a bear curved on the mouth of an unknown animal.

His second picture is a strong, even painful image – almost as if he has seen this happen. It is like an image in Edwin Muir's poem 'The Combat': 'The fury had him on his back'. Muir says in his autobiography that this came from a dream of two animals fighting. In a talk on images and symbols, Sir Kenneth Clark showed that the image of a strong animal preying on a weaker one occurs in the work of ancient and medieval artists, nineteenth century Romantic painting, and Picasso.

Christine's account of her writing may help to explain why the children wrote well for her. Things catch her eye when there is tension between their movement and their stillness – a cat, a hare, a fish; and when like the shell they contain or suggest some kind of life that can't be penetrated and so are 'secretive and mysterious'. The 'glimpses and instances' given by these are dynamic: the verb 'springs' in her first sentence shows this. Secrets and the drama of stillness and movement are dynamic also for children. When she talked with them about the shell she touched off these springs.

Most of my work springs from glimpses and instances. The poems are about moments that have crystallized. The object, the situation, or the time is seen out of the corner of my eye, and caught like an insect in amber.

I find that if I try to write a poem I very rarely succeed in saying what I mean. The poems I have written with an eye or ear on something else seem to get to the pivot of the experience without my looking for it. All the poems here are examples of this.

The one about the hare was written in ten minutes. I saw the hare from my window and doodled the poem on to the paper. Its present form is the same as the original.

The shell poem seemed to appear on the paper while I was trying out my new typewriter. I found the shell in a churchyard in Sussex five years ago, and kept it in a box at home. It seemed to me to be a real memorial; and although it was tiny in comparison with the surrounding gravestones, its beauty and simplicity meant more to me than all the words in 'In Memoriam'. It was secretive and mysterious, and evoked in me the kind of curiosity I felt about the people who lay buried in the churchyard.

I saw the cat in a field, sitting as though he was in front of the fire at home; and as soon as I saw him, the first verse came into my mind.

I find that I can write more easily when there is sound about me. If I have to labour over a poem I abandon it, or perhaps go back to it later. I don't take care over my work. If what I want doesn't happen at once, then I usually leave it – otherwise it may be out of tune.

UNDER THE GREEN WATER

Under the green water
I am a green fish,
warm as the waves
that cover me.

F

I can sweep down
to the hard floor,
or hang half-way,
resting on the water.

My hair swirls into my eyes,
and flows out like water-weed
taken in the current,
or streamers in the wind.

This is to fly,
to swim under water,
to arch and liquefy,
curl into the moving waves.

And when I shoot towards the air,
my head cracks the surface;
I come into the sky,
and burst the sun.


CAT
A ginger cat
sat in a field,
still, sculptured into the grass.

Unblinking eyes looked,
saw, undancing;
so cat-green and opal.

Hot flames
of purring fur
flickered inside cool blades

where it sat,
paws tucked under,
so smoothly deceptive.

Quietly regarding
fleeting birds;
secure as the sphinx.


A HARE
High up, on the hill,
a hare lollops
and stops,
then lollops again;
his legs surprising me
with their length,
his body with its speed.
Until he moves,
I cannot possibly
see where he sits.

He is merged, camouflaged,
with the soil colour
and the stones.
He goes again,
ears up, sharp;
eyes looking, beads
of brown brilliance.
Now the fur
streaks in the wind.
He's streamlined,
air-borne, and off
to the other side
of the world.

A SHELL
An empty shell,
dry; no soft slimy body
to slide slowly, smoothly
up and down grass and stone.
No tender eye to peep,
ponderously shy;
or recoil at the lightest touch,
the only sharp movement.
Now, still closed to the prying,
the shell speaks all;
as a delicate monument
among the greater stones.

# [ iv ] Plain Imagination

We have made some dyes they are called lichen dye and dandelion and leaf
dye and Iris root and rust dye. Pauls brother found the lichen on top of there
shed we boild them. In the lichen we found a spider we couled not take it out
and so we boild it with the lichen.    JONATHAN

### Bob

Bob, one of our older students taking a two-year course (pages
(32 to 35), worked with a class of six and seven year olds on his first
practice. Paul was one of them.

I noticed one small boy looking at me as if he wanted to tell me something.
He came up and held out a sticky lump of bees-wax that someone had given
him at the Bath and West Show. I told him I thought that bees-wax was used
to make shoe-polish. This caught his imagination. He devised a simple piece

of apparatus to melt down the wax. Then it had to be coloured. I suggested powder paint and left him to get on with it. This was no good, so I gave him a book on vegetable dyes and told him to find out as much as he could. It was a good deal to ask of a seven year old.

He kept up his experiments for the next four or five days. He had plenty of initiative and common sense, and would allow no practical difficulty to defeat him. On the second day we provided a saucepan and stove, and established him near the class teacher's table. I stayed with him whenever I could. Together we collected plants. He picked dozens of dandelion heads, and took rust from the school railings because the book said that it made a good red dye for the sails of fishing-boats. He also wanted some iris roots and lichen. I could see from the look in his eye that he was already thinking of places where he might find some. Next day he had a supply of both: his mother had dug up her iris roots, and his elder brother had climbed on to a roof to scrape lichen from the tiles. We boiled, strained, and filtered; then dyed samples of cloth in as many ways as we could.

Paul was the master mind behind all these activities. No doubt the support his family gives him spurs him on: nothing is too much trouble for them. He shows mature characteristics of enterprise, concentration, and determination.

When at last he was satisfied – almost a week later – he wanted to record the details of the processes he had tried out or discovered, and set up a display in the class-room. It was arranged in a corner, with his samples and jars of dyes properly labelled.

Though he expresses himself well in conversation, at the moment he is less happy with writing. This was his attempt:

'We made some dyes wiht licden iris roots and leeves and we boild them in a tin.'

Helpers had joined him from time to time, and he persuaded one of them, Jonathan, to do most of the writing for him.

The children's writing, in this instance, was far outstripped by their learning. But they had seen the point of writing; and they were using words that meant something to them.

Judith, another student in Bob's group, found out on her first practice that to ask children to 'pretend to be raindrops' is not the best way to help them to write imaginatively. A child has experience of his own to use. Can he be expected to know how a raindrop 'feels' – or even an insect or an animal, that is capable of feeling? Unless he learns from the outside that they feel in ways refreshingly different from ours, his trees and animals later on are going to be feeble projections of himself.

Coleridge's statement that it is an instinct of human nature to pass out of self and 'exist in the form of others' was based partly on his own experience at the age of six: '. . . I was accustomed to race up and down the churchyard, and act over all I had been reading on the docks, the nettles and the rank grass.' Infants will forget themselves as soon as they put on their dressing-up clothes, or they become, without effort, drops of rain in a thunderstorm or swirling mist, and may talk or write about their play. But without this experience they may not feel the impulse to sit down and put into words what their bodies will instinctively play out in movement. They may have too little knowledge to re-create. Behind the Indian dancer's peacock and Hardy's creation of Tess, there are years of exact learning and of practice in using a medium. After beginning her poem as a wave (page 61), it is a relief to Kim to write in her own person:

> . . . and I am
> paddling and my mummy and daddy are paddling and
> even my grandpa is paddling.

Heather has more immediate experience to sustain her, of waves rushing in, then thinning over the sand; the 'rustling' noise may have come from the sound she heard in a shell.

### Carolyn again

Carolyn writes, in her second year of teaching:

I've never suggested this way of beginning a description – thinking that it was outside the children's experience, and so not vital or interesting to them. But some of them, of their own accord, begin writing with the words, 'I am . . .'. Last year I noticed that the infants who had difficulty in expressing themselves used it as a starting-point: it was something definite, and they'd get it down on paper and then drift away from it towards the end. But this year, in my class of children between the ages of six and a half and nine, I've found the opposite: for instance, Matthew, who enjoys writing, has produced three consecutive pieces beginning, 'I am. . .'. In one he is a trapped snowflake wanting to escape from a snow-man, in another a fish taking the bait and being hauled into the sunlight. He wrote the first after a fall of snow, and the second after seeing a film about salmon:

'I am a fish. It is a bright summer morning and I am just going out for a swim. The water is especially nice and frothy. Look! There is a minnow! I will catch it! I have! Oh! A fly! I have caught it. Help! That fly is pulling upwards. I can't let go! I am in the sunshine!'

I've been thinking about this way of writing. 'I am' is one of the first things the infants write – 'I am six years old', 'I am in class 1'; and they're always using it in conversation. Many of the simpler poems in their books are forms of personification: flowers speak of pushing through the ground, trees of unfolding their leaves. I suppose that if the children hear or read the poems, this will strike them as something to be tried later. Matthew said, 'I wrote the poem with me instead of the fish because I wanted to try it out.' If someone in the group has an idea of this kind, others will want to follow. I think it more than likely that in one of my discussions with the infants on my last practice I may have asked something like, 'What do you think it feels like to be a wave struggling up the beach?'; and there is always a child ready to take up a suggestion.

Children have their own worlds. I'm continually learning that they can get outside themselves – outside the squabbles over who found a book first, or whose turn it is to hold the hamster – and realize that life isn't the same for everybody. Our hamster has been treated with rather more consideration since we tried to imagine what it would be like if a dinosaur picked us up by one leg and peered at us: this is more solid food for the children's thoughts and feelings than if I were to say, 'Don't be cruel – you'll hurt him!' It is a way of keeping their imagined experience in mind, and experimenting with it afterwards; I know this because they go home and ask their parents what they'd feel like in certain situations.

A child may sometimes find a real correspondence to express in writing: in a poem I have seen about the germination of a seed and its growth into a flower, a girl of ten has been able to describe her own experience of growth – that she is aware of in her feelings rather than her mind – by letting the seedling speak for her. The subject and treatment were not suggested by her teacher: she was accustomed to writing, and almost certainly her impulse was to describe the seedling's experience, not release her own. But a child responding to the words, 'Pretend you are . . .' may be playing with the 'counters' of fancy that remain 'fixities and definites', and not with experience that he is re-creating. There may be more material for the imagination to work on in a straight-forward recording of fresh experience. Bees, rust, lichen, iris, dandelion, and the sails of fishing boats, all came into Paul's experiments. Facts are taken in by primary imagination, 'the living Power and prime Agent of all human Perception'. Imagination is 'plain' in as much as its material is fact, taken in through the senses into the mind of a particular person.

I asked Carolyn if she would comment on her remark that the infants' writing was 'factual and positive rather than expressive'. She wrote:

'When they have an object in front of them, they would write down what was there. For example, "It is a hamster. It is brown. It has fur." They were making an effort, experimenting with vo-cabulary. But some of them – and this is what I want to encourage – would say things like "It is brown. My teddy bear has brown eyes"; "The hamster looks like fudge." The description is more significant; it is personal and lively. It is a link with past ex-perience.'

She knew that factual writing was 'positive', and important in its own right. She wanted to take the children further, to set their minds working even more energetically and release this energy in writing; to draw out primary imagination in its most active form – the perception that frees them from dependence on copying or repetition.

'I should like them to find their own words for describing things.' For her, this is a sign of imaginative writing, proof that the children have seen for themselves. In factual writing, a child, looking at what is in front of him, sees part of the truth about it, the part we all see more or less alike: 'It is brown. It has fur.' A simple instance of imaginative writing is Adrian's poem about a cone:

It feels like a hedhog
it is sharp and brown
It grows on a fat tree
Baby birds wont sit on the pricks
It smels like an elephant.

This is both practical and sensitive, exact and personal. Adrian has made a deduction and is concerned with what might happen, but the picture of a baby bird is unexpected; it wouldn't occur to every child who looks at a prickly cone. Most people would have described the tree as 'large' or 'spreading' rather than 'fat'. 'Fat' describes the way Adrian sees it; and it is the word one might use of some of the trees in paintings by Alfred Wallis. Wallis kept his vision fresh, as when he saw trees in childhood; he told H. S. Ede in a letter that most of what he painted came out of his own memory. Andrew (in a class taught by Christine) looks at a flower as if for the first time:

A flower is a funny thing,
Its head is yellow,
Its arms are green.

Steven in his poem about the cow (page 63),

This cow it is a she
and she makes a noise
like you eating lettuces
and she eats grass,

has taken in four facts with surprise and delight. Karen looking at the tulip (page 57) makes the 'link with past experience':

It is cold and smooth like hair
It could break
when the wind blows.

The words in these poems are used with their full value. The children are thinking not of readers but of the cone, the flowers, and the cow. They use their own words, and at this stage 'any word is exciting'.

To show what she means by expressive writing, Carolyn gives the example of imagery. An image is both factual and imaginative. Two experiences meet, one from the present and one from the past:

> . . . the leaf looks lick a
> chimmuny pot.

This is a description of a primula leaf. Images are individual; one child's experience isn't the same as another's. Blake wrote in his copy of Reynolds's *Discourses*: 'Every Eye sees differently. As the Eye, such the Object.' Half way through her first year of teaching, Carolyn said in a letter,

I have scribbled out the ideas flung at me by my class last week. We had found dew on the grass (miraculously preserved until 9 a.m.), and I asked, 'What does dew look like?' Straight away came the answers:

little clean snow-flakes
live thin snow-drops
icicles chopped off
fresh frozen crumbs of bread
dribbles from a baby
drops of rain
sugar grains stuck together
lace in frills
chalk dust on the floor
mushroom peelings
crumbs of white cheese
shiny silk
splashes in the bath
milk when it's spilled
bubbles from a straw
white feathers from a bird
the inside white of an egg
branches of white hay and straw
cobwebs tangled up
needles in a bundle.

(The last three describe the grass, not the dew.)

As soon as infants begin to paint, they paint imaginatively. But as a rule, when they begin to write they write factually. Before a child or anyone else can write imaginatively, there has to be what Coleridge describes as a 'confluence of recollections' in his mind. It may take time for the recollections to come together as they did in the poem about the waterfall on page 18. Andrew Marvell pictures this interval of their merging – the time between their entering the conscious mind and their shaping by imagination – in his image of a mind not quite active, not quite passive, being coloured and lit by shifting memories, like a bird withdrawn into the branches of a tree:

And, till prepar'd for longer flight,
Waves in its Plumes the various Light.

The things Carolyn had talked about with the infants before she asked them to write – dragons, the sea, salmon leaping, 'dewy grass growing in clumps' – were ones she herself had drawn on for images in her description of the rock. Like the square patches on the cliff face with small flowers and sea-gulls' eggs, they go back to her childhood:

The ledges on the cliff and the seagulls' eggs came from memories of the Gower coast, Pembrokeshire holidays, and the 'Wild Life' series of television films. At Saundersfoot when I was nine I fed a seagull and afterwards he used to tap my window every morning; I remember the surprise of realizing how big he was. The flowers were sea-pinks growing on rocks at Broadhaven; I must have seen them when I was seven. The salmon leaping came partly from *Salar the Salmon*, and from a film I once saw of the life cycle of a salmon. I have seen salmon leap in the Wye when I have been fishing with my father. We caught one near Brecon, but it was so small that we put it back.

An image comes spontaneously; the recollections that flow together are brought to the surface by involuntary memory rather than by a deliberate attempt to remember. They are set free, it seems, when a teacher's or a writer's imagination fuses with a child's. Though Anne never read to the children any part of the novels, Virginia Woolf's awareness of contrasts between day and night and of the free movement of light and water filtered down to them through her teaching, and released each child's memories. None of the poems about the shell would have been written if Christine hadn't found the snail shell and kept it for five years before she wrote about it. 'It seemed to me to be a real memorial

. . . and evoked in me the same kind of curiosity I felt about the people who lay buried in the graveyard.'

In her letter about the children's images Carolyn said, 'I began to wonder how much they were seeing things in my way. So many of the things they mentioned had already gone through my mind. This is a sobering thought.' She wanted their writing to be independent; eventually they would write on their own. I admired the work of my colleague who taught Alison, Diana, and Marie because his students' paintings never reflected a pattern that he had imposed. But I don't think Carolyn should be too much sobered by this thought. The images were drawn out by her pleasure in what she saw, and in sharing it with the children.

It is impossible to tell what happening, story, poem, picture, word, or music will seed itself in the mind of a child or a grown writer; and hard at times, if not impossible, to find the origins of symbols the imagination uses. A writer can sometimes trace recurrent symbols in his life and work to their sources, and see 'the relation between the patterns of his life and the themes of his writing' – as Angus Wilson has done in *The Wild Garden*.

## [v] Top juniors

### *Vic*

Vic was another of our older students. He had been a commercial artist, and his main subject was Design. On his final practice he took a class of forty-five top juniors. This was the spring term, and already there had been several changes of class teacher. He wanted the children to work more freely, in groups for part of the time, though it would have been easier to keep to conventional methods with a class of this size. For the first few weeks he got very little response.

He went on experimenting until the children had mastered certain techniques and were beginning to realize what could be done with different media. He gave them confidence in their abilities. As he says in his notes, the situation was 'fluid'. It took considerable courage not to compromise and teach in more formal ways. A younger student might have felt too insecure for this kind of teaching—always at risk, going over the same ground more than once, adapting his plans, scrutinizing their results, putting to immediate use what he found out from one day to the next.

His diary was full of queries, for example:

If the children had to ask questions to elicit information, then the information would take on an added meaning, and they might be more exacting in their demands for adequate answers. How can we achieve this?

In his first painting lesson, he found that most of the children would not begin to paint until they had drawn everything with a pencil, using rulers to get straight lines.

Their use of colour was highly factual. Some asked if they could use candle wax under the colour, but their efforts were restrained to the point of timidity. What can one do about this? The obvious answer would be to take their pencils away and give them as much painting as possible. But when they begin to paint, they should be trying to paint something they have felt strongly. The difficulty is to find the right kind of experience and to go on doing this until they feel the impulse to paint from their own experience.

Most of what he says about the children's work in design can be applied to their writing. Doing without rhyme, and using the images that occurred to them when they looked at clouds or guinea pigs or visualized the people in the Square gave them the same kind of freedom as working in paint or brilliant crayons without a pencilled outline:

Puf puf go the chimneys of the houses as the
houses go out.

### *Sometime we see a cloud that's dragonish*

Verity in a letter sent to the Channel Islands spoke of Bath as being like a pudding-basin. I want to do some work which will encourage the children to use similes and metaphors.

The subject should give opportunities for both accurate observation and imaginative interpretation. We will go into the playground and look at clouds; we will try to describe them there: using metaphors and similes as often as possible, as it seems that these fire the imagination.

In the classroom we will consolidate our observations, and record them. Then I shall ask the children to write prose or verse descriptions.

At last we have had the right kind of day for looking at clouds. It is very difficult to maintain the interest of the whole class when there are so many of them.

First we talked about colour. They kept calling the clouds 'grey'; but when I pressed them, they said, 'burnt grey', 'pearly grey'. With shapes they were more imaginative: angels, horses, the British Isles, were all seen in the clouds. Rosalind said the texture was like a poodle's fur.

For some time, Nicholas has been asking if he could bring in his two guinea pigs; and I arranged that this should happen on Monday.

Celia held one, and Nicholas the other. The children were absorbed, and wanted only to look. I waited for a few minutes for them to enjoy the situation, then they gave me descriptions of colour, shape, position, and movement. One of the guinea pigs had that uncomfortable, undecided kind of fur that lies both backwards and forwards, with short haphazard partings. Verity said that it looked as if it had been back-combed, and Anne thought the clusters looked like rosettes. There was too little time for all forty-five of us to look as closely as we needed to.

### *There was an old dragon under grey stone*

In one lesson, I read the description of Smaug, out of *The Hobbit*. In the next, the children wrote about a dragon – their own dragon, as it were.

They remembered Smaug very well, and offered plenty of words when I asked for descriptions, such as 'bony', 'scaly', 'fat' (this would describe a friendly dragon). When we came to colour, I asked if they could suggest words that would also indicate the kind of texture or surface; one gave me 'brilliant green', but most of them kept to plain colour names.

In their writing, livelier expressions appeared. I read of 'gleaming gold', 'slimy green'. The dragon was 'brown as mud', and smelled 'like mouldy cloth'. His perch in the 'cold wet cave' was 'a mound of gravel'. His skin was 'tough as old boots' and 'thick as the leg of a grown man', his body 'scarred, as if many men had tried to kill him'; he 'waddled' when he walked; and the treasure 'was sparkling like the sun in the early hours of the morning'.

While they are interested, I shall have the children draw a dragon in coloured crayons, using their descriptions as a guide – that is, if they want to: I must avoid giving the impression that the picture must tally with the description.

I shall provide as many pictures as I can of dinosaurs, lizards, and bats, making sure that the children look at them once; after that, I don't mind if they ignore them. I think one has to go on working in this way until they begin to look for themselves.

I will read the description of griffins in *Come Hither*.

We used the Jumbo crayons. The children discovered that if they put the paper on the worn surfaces of the desks and rubbed with the crayon, this gave an interesting texture. Repeated with more colours, the design became even richer and more satisfying.

The two most pleasing aspects of this lesson were the intensity with which the colour was applied (this came after a good deal of coaxing), and the freedom of the drawing. I made the children work straight away with the crayon: the result was a spontaneity that so far has been missing from their attempts.

This morning I talked about their dragons, trying to make my central point their contrasts in colour, tone, or shape. Then I pinned up six or seven of them together with a few of their written descriptions.

*The golden sun . . .*
          *. . . carbuncle most or chrysolite,*
*Ruby or topaz . . .*

I wanted the children to do as much work as possible with the crayons. These are so big and their colours so bright that it comes naturally to work freely with them. We looked at pictures of the sun – both scientific and imaginative. The children thought of words to describe its qualities, then began to draw.

The results were not as exciting as I had hoped they would be, though for a trial run the work was encouraging. On the whole it was uninventive; it reflected their lack of experience in using the crayons, and also in thinking imaginatively about something that is usually looked on as a scientific phenomenon. It would be an interesting experiment to talk to them beforehand about this first set of drawings, and then to give almost exactly the same lesson as before.

The suns, when I put them up, seemed to belie my earlier remarks; but I think this is only because a number of suns make more impact than one at a time.

I realize more and more that the best work is done in lessons that have grown out of experience in a different medium. The dragon drawings are a case in point: they grew from the poems and descriptions. Having expressed themselves in one medium with some degree of success, the children feel impelled to pursue the same subject in another medium.

One has to remember that for them success means a piece of writing that is finished. It is best not to be too preoccupied with quality in so short a period as a teaching practice. We must not look at the children as artists, authors, mathematicians: this is a trap that it is only too easy to fall into.

Also, one tends to think that when a lesson based on a good idea has disappointing results one should abandon the idea; and when a lesson has gone well we say, 'That's that! Now we must think of something else.' We should be prepared for plenty of repetition. Most subjects involve the learning of a technique, and until the child has some competence in using the technique his ideas will be only half expressed.

*The dancers are all gone under the hill*
          *Fishes*
*With their gold, red eyes, and green-blue gleam, and under gold.*

First group: Modelling fish in clay. We have plenty of reference books to use. The children have already painted an underwater scene, and I shall try to move on from this.

Second group: I have found a big piece of fibre board. This morning before coming to school I made a chain of paper figures for my son Justin. It struck me that this idea could be developed in the classroom, using not only chains of people, but also chains of houses, chains of trees. The theme can be 'Dancing in the Square'. I will try to use part of the dinner hour to explain what I want the children to do.

Third group: Two boys, Graham and Julian. (Both these children have difficulties at the moment.) Two days ago they were playing with plasticine; each has developed a small motif, which can be taken further. I have given them each a fibre board to work on, surrounded by a picture frame. I am hoping that a relationship, however small, will develop between them while they are working together.

I met the paper-chain people at one o'clock, and explained what I had in mind for them. In the afternoon I was able to concentrate first of all on the children working in clay; once these were started, I went to the others. Four were painting the board: blue sky, green ground. Others cut out houses, trees, dancers, people watching, dogs and cats. We have only white, off-white, and grey paper for the figures.

We may be able to do some writing on this subject of dancing in the Square.

Graham and Julian are working at their clay motifs. Julian is producing designs that look like the cross-section of a complex plant stalk; I must talk to him about this when he has a little more done.

I got Alliston and Verity to hold up the board. I asked, 'Where's the music coming from? I can't see a band!' Alliston said it came from a barrel organ. We talked about the dancing figures, and I asked for all the words they could think of to describe the movements of dancing. They thought of 'twirling', 'waltzing', 'spinning', etc. I asked them how a hefty butcher would dance – not so much for an answer, as to open their minds to the idea of all sorts of people dancing. We talked about the houses: they all had a deserted look.

I read 'The Piper' by Seumas O'Sullivan.

Several children asked to be allowed to write a prose description rather than a poem.

Their first poems were based on rather lifeless generalities, and the rhymes were forced. I asked them to forget that there was such a thing as rhyme, and tried to help them to think of the characters who lived in the Square, and how they would dance.

I am beginning to see that while good preparation and stimulus are essential, the real teaching begins once the children start writing. It is not until they are actively writing that one can come to terms with what is being given out.

One boy's poem:

> All the people are shouting and singing
> The barrel organ is here
> Horay horay shout the children
> Horay horay shout the children
> Meaw say the cats
> Puf puf go the chimneys of the houses as the
> houses go out.
>
> The dancing goes on and on.
> The fires go out
> The sun has set
> The lights go on
> The dancing has stopped
> The dancers have gone have gone have gone.

I wanted to show the children how exciting effects can be produced by painting over a texture drawn in either candle wax or Jumbo crayon. I suggested that they drew a pattern in crayon and then painted over it. They took 'pattern' to mean a formal repetitive design. I should have talked to them about texture and discussed real textures – rock, sand, waves, plumage. I was able to recapture the lesson by changing the idea of pattern to that of texture. They had another go, with fresh paper and better results.

A further attempt at producing these textures was much more successful. It was as if the period between the two lessons had given the children an understanding of what they were trying to do.

The situation is fluid; and I was in some doubt as to what I should do in the next lesson. However, events conspired to supply me with the answer.

I had been trying to prepare the children for a more direct approach to painting by having them work with water colour over wax or crayon. I suddenly realized that this water colour and crayon would be an ideal medium for painting fish. The clay fish the boys had made have been admired by the rest of the class.

I read part of 'The Forsaken Merman' and a poem about water, then I showed the children some pictures, emphasizing that in painting fish the texture was important. I asked them to paint as large as possible. Then I was able to show the technique to the ones who hadn't taken part in the earlier experiment.

I think the real value of the lesson lay in their enjoyment of it. They were tackling a new field of activity, trying to master a new technique, and at the same time endeavouring to control the technique to produce an image. Hard work, in fact.

'. . . when they begin to paint, they should be trying to paint something they have felt strongly. The difficulty is to find the right kind of experience, and to go on doing this until they feel the impulse to paint from their own experience.' This seems to me to get to the heart of the matter – as far as children and teachers are concerned who are not too rigidly bound by the pattern of a syllabus.

What Vic says about this need to paint something felt strongly, and about the need for repetition ('It was as if the period between had given the children an understanding of what they were trying to do') is borne out by the experience of some seven year olds at the school where Peter and Bob were attached to parallel classes on their first practices. Peter outlined the shape of a fish with flies he used for bait. This delighted the children. Then he asked them to draw some fish. The drawings were disappointing stereotypes. When their Headmistress heard about the fish outlined in flies, she called the school together and on three days in succession they sat in the hall and listened to Schubert's *Trout* Quintet. During these three days a collection was assembled of fishing tackle, books about fish, books about Schubert, a violin, and other musical instruments. Two of the girls in Bob's class asked if they could dance to the music. They planned their dance at home, and when it was ready other classes took it in turn to watch, sitting in a circle with the girls dancing in the middle. After this Peter asked his class to paint fish. Their paintings were of a quite different quality from their earlier drawings – inventive, varied, full of life.

I asked Vic if he would comment on his remark about the children's paintings: 'Their use of colour was highly factual.' This is his answer:

Children are welded firmly into their environment and experience, and this is never more clearly seen than in painting or writing. Whether a child writes factually about his imaginings, or imaginatively about his facts, what he writes must in the first instance come from his experience. Gnomes and goblins are just as much reality to the five or six year old as a visit to Heathrow airport is to the twelve year old. Unfortunately, the twelve year old's reality has a physical existence which the five or six year old's has not: a physical existence which allows it to be touched, measured, and, in a sense, possessed. I say 'unfortunately', because far too many people never get beyond enslavement to the existence of things. The very existence of a thing reassures: if it *is*, then I *am*.

When the children were using colour factually, I found it extremely difficult to get them to take experience, assimilate it, and reproduce it creatively.

As an adult, I would paint or model factually, then repeat and repeat my attempts until I began to break free from the original matrix, hoping to produce something that had never existed before. I have had too little experience to know whether it is possible to help children to do this. I certainly intend to try.

When a child produces a painting which to our adult eyes carries all the exciting distortions and colour contrasts that make us think of it as imaginative, it may well be that he is disappointed with his effort, and that the image to which he was aspiring, a far more mundane and 'realistic' one, was too difficult for his limited technique to convey. This is a further snare when one is trying to represent physical reality – it is a thing so difficult to do, that it becomes a challenge!

### Anne

At the end of their second year, students taking the main English course begin to read for a long essay to be written on a subject of their own choice. They have to finish it before the end of the first term of the third year, then prepare for their final teaching practice after Christmas.

Anne wrote on Virginia Woolf. The images used in the novels, of time and renewal, sparked off constructive ideas that she was able to use with the children (ten and eleven year olds). The writing they did for her reflects their enjoyment of the life, movement, and change in things around them:

. . . and the sun is going on the grasses of the spiked and smooth. And the water of the earth is cascading on the land, the smooth of the tree is the sun and sunset of the day.   DAVID

The ladies take the gay flowers out of their hair. The rhythm is no longer heard in the village but is heard in the hills.   JANE

My interest in Virginia Woolf began with a talk I gave to the English group in our first year. I chose her for my subject because I had been reading *To the Lighthouse* and was enthralled and puzzled. In S Level classes at school we had spent just enough time on her to arouse my curiosity. I wanted to work out the problems for myself.

I knew that there was a fathomless sea of imagery in her novels: the essay gave me the opportunity to explore it.

In the vacation at the end of the second year I re-read the novels, with the time theme in my mind. I kept discovering all kinds of other subjects connected with time. When I had made countless notes, a pattern began to emerge; then I shaped, pared, extended my material. By feeling the pulse of the essay in my mind as each section took shape, I began to understand the discipline of writing. It was like setting out to reclaim a polder. I wrote most of my chapters at least twice. I sometimes had to leave the essay for several days, or for a week, before I was able to look at it as a whole.

These paragraphs on the seasons come from the fourth of Anne's five chapters.

### Time Symbols

In her Diary, Virginia Woolf writes of *The Waves*,
    '. . . this shall be childhood; but it must not be *my* childhood . . . the sense of children; unreality; things oddly proportioned . . . the unreal world must be round all this – the phantom waves.' But the world she refers to here as 'unreal' is, for her, the essential reality; '. . . and nothingness only comes in the absence of this'.

In exploring Virginia Woolf's images in the novels, I am indebted to the work of Jean Guignet, who first made their depth apparent to me; but I should like to point out before I begin that I intend to tackle them from a different angle, as symbols of time.

The seasons and elements in *The Voyage Out* are often associated with dramatic moments. For instance, the marvellous autumn lengthened by the eternal sunshine of Santa Maria symbolizes a time of postponement and blossoming. This is taken further in the later novels.

In *Mrs Dalloway*, the summertime of Peter Walsh's memories is an image of his love for Clarissa. He remembers arriving at dawn on a fine morning. The present time, the day of Clarissa's party, is a perfect summer day: baskets of flowers swing in doorways, blinds are not drawn until the last moment. 'Like the pulse of a perfect heart, life struck straight through the streets. There was no fumbling – no hesitation.'

Summer gluts the beginning of *The Waves*, where the six children play in the garden before lessons. Descriptions of the freshness and fertility of nature show that Virginia Woolf saw their childhood as a time of discovery. Bernard says, 'Now, let us explore.' The sun streaking through the warm leaves and dancing 'on the tips of the flowers' 'made the garden like a mosaic of single sparks not yet formed into one whole'; scissors were incessantly clipping roses; oak apples, 'red with age and slippery', were squelching into the grass; ferns smelled strong in the warmth, and a toad flopped in the undergrowth. All this filled the children with wonder and delight: 'We are the discoverers of an unknown land.'

In *To the Lighthouse*, summer symbolizes both death and permanence. It is during this season that Prue dies in childbirth. The summer after the ten-year lapse during which Mrs Ramsay dies represents the triumph of duration over time, even over death. Mrs Ramsay, who died within time, haunts these pages with a presence that echoes the material permanence of the lighthouse itself.

The height of summer in three chapters of *The Years* represents a period of suspension for the people involved in them. For Martin, in 1907, it marks his transition from India and Africa to England. As he sits outside on a romantic summer night at Wapping, at an inn where 'each table has its pyramid of strawberries, its pale plump quail', the warmth and comfort seem to suck him once more into the continuity of life in England.

The single June day in 1939 shown in *Between the Acts* provides a backcloth of continuity and unity for the pageant and for the lives of individuals watching it, each belonging to a different world, seldom uniting; while behind it there is the horror of the dark night that covers Europe: for the Rev. G. W. Streatfield, for instance, 'ignored by the cows, condemned by the clouds which continued their majestic rearrangement of the celestial landscape; an irrelevant forked stake in the flow and majesty of the summer silent world'.

I know very little about Virginia Woolf's summers as a child; but her Diary discloses the intensity with which she lived during her summers on the downs at Rodmell, and in Cornwall. A summer at Rodmell eased her mind after exhausting stretches in London, where she did most of her writing. In her entry for Saturday August 20th 1932, she longs for its warmth and security to last: 'I believe I want this more humane state of existence for my next – to spread carelessly among one's friends – to feel the width and amusement of human life . . . to let the juice of usual things, talk, character, seep through me . . .' She records her relief on entering the peace of the countryside in summer: 'Coming back we had the car shut and the windscreen open – thus sat in a hot rough gale which, as we came to the lanes and woods, became deliciously cold and green.' She delighted in a fox nosing its way into the furze, a weasel crossing a race-course, a mole gliding over a meadow, '. . . and that fading and rising of the light which so enraptures me in the downs'. Summer is dominated by 'a feeling of washing in boundless warm fresh air'. The Sussex countryside where she spends her summers takes its place not only as a setting, but as an infinite source of images seeking to reveal to her the truth behind life. It is '. . . too much for one pair of eyes. Enough to float a whole population in happiness, if only they would look.'

T. S. Eliot uses images of summer in 'East Coker' to suggest a state of ecstasy:

> The wild thyme unseen and the wild strawberry,
> The laughter in the garden, echoed ecstasy . . .

These images drawn from summer are images of the moment, presenting reality.

In 'Little Gidding', the last of the Quartets, winter is the renewer of life; it is through experience of this season, when time and the timeless intersect, that life is re-born:

> This is the spring time
> But not in time's covenant. Now the hedgerow
> Is blanched for an hour with transitory blossom
> Of snow, a bloom more sudden
> Than that of summer . . .

Little Gidding is 'A symbol perfected in death'. In the novels of Virginia Woolf, this time of year symbolizes disillusionment, suffering, and death – even though it could be a period of fulfilment in personal life. Her entry in her Diary on January 26th 1940 describes the cruelty of winter:

'. . . the lyric mood of the winter – its intense spiritual exaltation – is over. The thaw has set in; and rain and wind; and the marsh is soggy and patched with white, and two very small lambs were staggering in the east wind. One dead ewe was being carted off; and shirking the horror I crept back by the hanger.'

This cruelty does not appear in *The Voyage Out*, where 'the change of season from winter to spring had made very little difference', or in *Night and Day*, where winter is a period of doubt and despair for the lovers, dispelled by the too early spring. In *Jacob's Room* the first real Woolfian winter appears, a season when life retires into itself. Each moment seems to be separated from the next by immobility. 'At six o'clock a man's figure carrying a lantern crossed the field . . . A raft of twigs stayed upon a stone, suddenly detached itself, and floated towards the culvert. . . . A load of snow slipped and fell from a fir branch. . . . Later there was a mournful cry. . . .' Winter becomes the night of the year, a foretaste of death. It is the season of old Crosby, the Pargiters' maid in *The Years*. The snow begins, sprinkling her bonnet as she climbs into the carriage with Rover in her arms, having said goodbye to the family. There was the little garden in which they used to plant crocuses. 'The grass was white; the trees were white; the railings were white; the only marks in the whole vista were the rooks . . .' Everything loses its identity as Crosby is torn from her life with the family. Even Rover changes. His impudence becomes indifference, and after three days of nursing he dies.

In *The Waves* spring represents the youth of the six characters: 'a bud here and there split asunder and shook out flowers, green veined and quivering, as if the effort of opening had set them rocking . . .'

Spring and autumn are seasons of wind and rain, buds bursting, dead leaves crumpled and drifting, tossed clouds, swirling birds, unstable temperatures, and turbulent skies. These seasons are not Virginia Woolf's favourites; they made her aware of the lapse of time and of life. They were hostile seasons. In spring she would break off work and go abroad. In April and October she usually suffered from head-aches and depression: '. . . . I doubt that I can write to any purpose. A cloud swims in my head.' It was in Spring that she killed herself.

After finishing my essay, I began my final teaching practice at a school on a new estate.

Some of the children had already been to as many as eight schools. They were unstreamed; one boy could do in five minutes what others took the best part of a day to finish.

I wanted to study *time* with the children: its history; the seasons; night and day; light and shadow; planets, astronomy and astrology. I set up a light experiment table; and the children devised and recorded their experiments and followed up the answers to their own questions. We discussed the effect of the seasons on animal, bird, flower, and tree cycles; ways of telling the time through the ages; the calendar; the origins of festivals in this country and abroad; the international date-line. This led the boys on to individual and group topics such as ways of telling the time at sea, the influence of the moon on the tides, and electrical timing devices.

We used different media to learn the effects of tones of colour, light and shadow on shapes of various kinds: wood shapes, pebble pots, spinning with wools we had dyed (yellow and red for sunrise and sunset, blue for daylight, black for the starred sky), and mobiles connected with space and time (a rocket, a dinosaur, planets, summer and winter shapes).

I wanted to help the children develop a sense of the past. We read legends connected with the seasons, and Alan Garner's *Elidor* because it introduces a journey into the past. I planned to build up scenes by using mime: children exploring an unknown land; the sensation of treading in water, and on sand and pebbles; climbing rocks into a strange castle and moving through mysterious rooms; an old fiddler, bent and hoary, his stick tapping. When I asked them to write anything other than stories, the children seemed to be at a loss, and it was only after a long discussion that they saw what I wanted them to do. None of them found it easy to write in verse form.

We began to talk about rhythm, and the sounds we had made playing the instruments in the classroom (drums, tambourines, threaded beech-nuts, shakers, and castanets). Afterwards we climbed a muddy lane over styles and across fields to the top of a hill, talking about things we found on the way like mole-hills, herbs and flowers (the children had never seen a speedwell before), and collecting grasses and leaves – spiky, curled, round. We heard sounds of gun-shot, farm noises, birds through trees, voices carried on the wind; and made lists of these on the spot. When we got back we talked about all these, and mounted or sketched the leaves and grasses.

Later, using the idea Sybil Marshall describes in *An Experiment in Education,* we listened to the Pastoral Symphony, a movement at a time. I played the first movement to try to evoke a feeling for the countryside, tranquillity,

the sky, colour, light. I didn't tell the children what Beethoven was describing
in each movement. We linked the sounds and the feelings they gave us with
our experiences on the walk. We talked about water, the sun after rain, and
the movement of grasses; and asked what shepherds' pipes would sound like
in the distance. I gave the children some bark to handle. Then I told them the
names of the movements. We heard the music again, and contrasted each
movement with the one before.

Everyone made his list of precise words, and began to write. Some
children needed a good deal of individual attention. Anthea's rough notes
read like poetry, and after some encouragement she read them out as free
verse. I was surprised to see that Steven had used such words as 'potion',
'orchestra', 'mellow pipes of shepherds'.

They read their efforts to one another, and talked about them freely. Then
we all listened to them and pooled our ideas. A child would say, 'I don't like
that bit', or ask, 'What does it mean?'; then we would discuss whether a
particular word sounded right, and try to find an alternative. Some would
accept suggestions, and alter their poems accordingly; others thought for
themselves. I tried to convince them that their sentences should be concise,
and move swiftly; and after a while many of them were trimming their
writing themselves. Practically everyone attempted a second draft, and they
all made neat copies and illustrated them.

> The clouds are like snow
> the butterflies sit on the swaying flowers
> shadows of the giant trees shake on the grass.
> the hills on the horizon stretching for miles.    LYNNE

> The rippling of the blue water
> the snow white mountains in the distance
> see the gob of fire in the sky.

> The clouds drifting in the sky
> The water cresded grass the sarp
> bladed grass and the jagged grass.

> The wasps busing and the bees busing
> carring there Queen, and see all the
> cows and sheep in there fields.

> The ponys galloping in there fields
> galloping bravely over the pools
> the brown ponys and the white ponys.

> the beautiful paralell trees in the distance
> the grompelled bark the sredded bark you see
> the cows eat there juicy grass.    MYRA

Myra had great difficulty with her spelling. She read her poem without
faltering. She was able to communicate her thoughts in this way. I decided
against encouraging her to alter the spelling, as it would change her contribution so drastically. We spent some time discussing the need to communicate
in our poems.

'The sky is the god of light, and the sunlight is going on the grasses of the spiked and smooth. And the water of the earth is cascading on the land the smooth of the tree is the sun and the sunset of the day. And animals are running in the woodlands of the Earth and the hedgehog and the fox is running on the land of the Earth in the sunlight of the day and in the night.'

DAVID

David was an athletic boy. He was small, wiry, over-anxious, and talkative. He read this piece beautifully. I asked him if he realized how like parts of the Old Testament his writing sounded.

> In the countryside you can see
> the crooked trees.
> and hear the spotted woodpecker
> pecking at the bark.
>
> In a field near by is a dappled mare,
> with a little black foal at her side.
> They canter around and around the field.
>
> At last all grows dim and silent,
> and not a sound is heard.
> You look up at the high green hill
> And see the silhouettes of
> old and humble cottages
> and the big and high church spire.     ANGELA
>
> Trees of all shapes
> Crowd the green meadow.
> Clouds flowing past.
> The river is deep.     MELINDA

These sentences describe the country people in the evening:

'One man finishes his cider with a big gulp, leaps into the middle of the room and starts dancing.'

'I grabbed a pink ribbon and twirled around.'

'The old men smoke and clap until their hands sting.'

'When the sunset came in the evening the noise died down and the music stopped playing. The people stop dancing, the children stop skipping. The ladies take the gay flowers out of their hair. The rhythm is no longer heard in the village but is heard in the hills.'

## [ vi ] Whole Sensibility

The infants have been listening to the story of Jason handle and smell the wool, and wonder why it is oily; they picture the shearing as something cruel and tragic, and ask for reassurance;

experience imaginatively the dragon's size and noise, and discover from the music that he can be enjoyed as well as feared.

The writing of seven year olds reflects the vitality of their learning experience. It makes you see and feel:

> The sea is wet blue green and salty.
> When I come out my skin tastes salty.[1]

Their bodily and mental energies are working not separately but together. When they describe exactly, it is with an active verb:

> Scrunch goes the cow.

Bruce thought ahead of his age group when he made his general qualified remark that tulips can be 'almost any colour'.[2] In his next piece of writing, he went back to particular facts and his own imagery:

> It is like a gun
> it is ruff
> it is blak brown.

A good deal of the writing done in fifth and sixth forms and by students in colleges and universities is general and impersonal – though not in the positive way that a scientist's writing is impersonal. The students and children have had to make the transition from immediate to abstract and general experience. What they write about is no longer their own experience. It has come to be detached from feelings and sensations. The writing is negative, faceless, a substitute for the writing of an individual.

As a rule, infants are not interested in qualifying a colour, or in describing a thing faithfully (in the usual sense of this word). One kind of blue is enough. Daffodils can be red or purple, and needn't have trumpets. Here again, Bruce was exceptionally objective and careful:

> It is blak brown.

The ten and eleven year olds record qualities, precisely:

> The colour of it is a greenish yellow . . .
> It is slimy yet beautiful.

This balanced observation has developed from something like the infant's simple way of looking:

> It is brown. It has fur.

[1] Writing done by infants for the Swindon women students.
[2] See p. 58.

These older children are writing out of their enjoyment of facts, or of imagined facts made from real ones. They are more detached than the infants – detached in mind, though not in feeling. Their thoughts and feelings still suffuse one another, so that they 'feel their thought' as immediately as the smell of a rose.[1]

[1] T. S. Eliot, 'The Metaphysical Poets' (in *Selected Essays*).

# 5  Thinking and feeling
*criticism*

... when I wrote it, it was a regular stepping of
the Imagination towards a Truth.    KEATS *Letters*

## [ i ] Understanding

The unthrift Sunne shot vitall gold
A thousand peeces,
And heaven its azure did unfold
Chequr'd with snowie fleeces ...

The image is brilliant and rich and overflowing. The dazzling gold is set
off by the blue with its design of cool white clouds. There is a magnitude and
richness here, like the richness of a feast.

Here Valerie, a first-year student, is re-creating Henry
Vaughan's experience in the mysterious poem 'Regeneration': an
explosion of joy, with the solemnity – 'the magnitude and richness' – of a feast. She 'feels' his thought, and there is feeling in her
own thought. Her description of the imagery shows that she has
absorbed the poem in the way Keats recommended, in a letter to
Reynolds, '... let him on a certain day read a certain page ... and
let him wander with it, and muse upon it, and reflect upon it, and
bring home to it ...'
  She understands a part of what Vaughan is saying, and her
words prepare me for his central experience, though they could
never express it entirely; only the poem can do this. Vaughan's
meaning will not be tempted into anyone else's words.
  Students attempting criticism of a poem, play, or novel are
exploring something new and separate. They have not watched it
grow and cannot know how the experiences it concentrates have
come together. Every attempt is a raid on meanings that are out of
their reach. One has to find ways of changing attitudes they have

acquired, of persuading them that they are writing not to enlighten anyone else, to praise, or to blame: but to learn for themselves.

As they go through the motions of 'critical appreciation', they write in desperate clichés:

> The words are so apt.
> The resulting description is very fitting.
> It is through the medium of his poetry that such sensations as these are made part of our heritage.
>
> He displays perception in the former poem.

A more common device is the pin-pointing of the absolute stillness of the surrounding countryside by describing one faint sound.

It is as if Sue, making the last two statements (in her first year), is insensitive to the meanings of the words 'display' and 'device'; but they are not her words – her thoughts, while they are forming, dress themselves up in what seems to be acceptable jargon.

> Movement and stillness he uses equally well.
> He applies the same aptitude of description to the movement of trees and grasses.

> Water movement has been observed and put into the poem. 'The poet' is fitting together spare parts of a poem in a kind of limbo.

> 'The choral minstrelsy' has been enjoyed.
> Sunlight itself is not neglected; it gives rise to the beautiful lines . . .

Coleridge climbing, looking, listening, writing, vanishes into passive verbs; and Sue, using her own mind, into the anonymous 'we': 'We feel that this comes from actual experience.'[1]

Most first-year students have been taught to use 'we', or 'the reader', rather than 'I'. They prefer passive to active verbs, abstract nouns to verbs and adjectives. The same formulas come in essay after essay: 'It is the verb "spot" that conveys so well . . .'

Though writing of this kind seems to move Sue further and further away from her meeting-point with Coleridge, there are signs in her essay that a relationship is growing up between his

---

[1]                         . . . the bat
Wheels silent by, and not a swallow twitters,
Yet still the solitary humble bee
Sings in the bean flower!

mind and hers. In one paragraph she is writing about some lines in the first verse of 'Dejection':

> This night, so tranquil now, will not go hence
> Unroused by winds, that ply a busier trade
> Than those which mould yon cloud in lazy flakes . . .

'Ply' conjures up the idea of winds as busy merchant ships marshalling the clouds, chasing them here and there. 'Mould' is an altogether slower, more deliberate movement: these winds can shape the clouds at leisure. One word has caught the implications of the movement Coleridge had seen. In 'The Eolian Harp' a slow cloud movement of a different kind is described: 'And watch the clouds that late were saddening round . . .' Here the stately measured turning of the cloud-bank is captured in the word 'saddening'. It carries the implication of approaching darkness. Yet another slow movement, this time a lazy one, is used of the breeze that touches the harp: 'How by the desultory breeze caress'd . . .' The touch is almost negligible, it is so light. A caress is with the fingertips, the most sensitive part of the hand. A desultory touch would be casual and passing. How explicit these two words make the description of the movement!

Here Sue is thinking and connecting for herself, opening her mind to the possible meanings in the words, and learning to distinguish between different shades of meaning. Her English is more positive and less stilted. There are fewer passive verbs. She is discovering how sharply Coleridge notices the things around him, how precise his words are.

What she says about the meanings of 'mould' and 'ply' suggests that, whether or not this was part of his intention, his images point forward. In the body of the poem his inner 'shaping spirit of Imagination' is almost passive, like the breath moulding the cloud-flakes, and without conscious will; in contrast to the creative life of the storm wind that is brewing outside. Her comments show this glimmer of insight into the nature of her subject: 'Coleridge's observation of nature, and its connection with his thoughts' (her own choice of subject). At this stage she was not able to go further. But by her third year she had learned from her own experience of writing that images drawn from observation might be very closely connected with thoughts. She says in her long essay that the image 'can mould your vague conceptions', and that it 'helps the poet to discover something'.

The origins of Romantic ideas may seem to be in Rousseau's philosophy. Man had discovered nature, a tract of experience of which eighteenth century man had seen little.

The landscape which Coleridge describes in 'Reflections on having left a Place of Retirement' is typical of the landscape described by the Romantic poets.

The students who made these generalizations need a strong dose of scepticism. What *are* these Romantic ideas? What is meant by the words 'may seem to be'? What has this to do with Coleridge, the subject of the essay? In what sense can man be said to have 'discovered' nature? What is meant here by 'man'? What by 'nature'? Did eighteenth century people really see so little of it? Where, in the poems of Keats, Byron, Shelley, or Wordsworth, is this kind of landscape to be found?

They need to be trained to 're-create' as truthfully as they can what they read on a printed page. Whoever wrote the third of these sentences implies that a certain kind of Romantic landscape was available for Coleridge to use; so that he was not writing of any place in particular. She has 'read' the poem without seeing what he saw so distinctly when he got to the top of the hill above his cottage at Clevedon on the Bristol Channel: round him, the rock 'speckled thin with sheep' – bare and bleak after the little wood behind him that refreshed his eyes with its greenness; then the Channel, with 'dim coasts and cloud-like hills'. The hill-top may have reminded her of the rocky place round Michael's sheep-fold in Wordsworth's poem. Perhaps her generalization, pushed to its limits to include all the Romantic poets, made her feel more secure; but it takes her nowhere. A comparison with Wordsworth might have started fresh trains of thought.

'Histories of Literature' lay formal patterns of centuries and 'movements' on something that, outside their pages, grows in its own way. Students want to generalize and classify where there is no pattern except the order made by individual writers out of their lives, in particular novels, poems, and plays. In time they may discover that they are seeing a writer differently in different parts of his work. Then a word like 'typical' may limit both themselves and him. It implies that they have exhausted his subtleties, and take him for granted; that he has to be consistent; that his character as a writer has crystallized in the moment of writing.

Blake says in his notes to Sir Joshua Reynolds's *Discourses*: 'Unless you Consult Particulars you Cannot even Know or See Mich. Ango. or Rafael or any Thing Else'; and Paul Klee in his Diary: 'I want to know . . . the tone of a particular work . . . I want to find out . . . just what is good about this particular work. I don't want to examine the common features of a series of works, or the difference between two sets of works – no such pursuit of history for me – but to consider the individual act in itself.'

Turner, who admired Reynolds, makes this comment on the remark in Opie's lectures that a student of art must not be content with a superficial survey, but must study attentively 'the peculiar manner of each master': 'Every glance is a glance for study . . . and develops by practice what appears to be mysterious.' According to Turner, 'Each tree and blade of grass or flower' is what it is, only 'in relation to the whole'. This strikes the balance between particular and general: for the painter and the writer, and for the critic.

It is not enough to show that Blake, Klee, and Turner said these things. They said them in the confidence of first-hand knowledge; and this is the very thing that an unsure student lacks. He has to be reassured. He has to produce something that he and his tutor both recognize as a development, an advance from his last piece of writing. It can be the same with a child and a teacher (Malcolm and Edith) – and with a seasoned writer waiting for notices, or for the most dreaded of all criticism – a friend's. What a student has learned, in the course of writing an essay, about his author and about his own mistakes, can matter less to him than the grade he is given afterwards. When he knows that the tutor has confidence in him, he will face criticism, and may act on it. High, low, average marks and grades, though useful to examiners, do nothing to develop his capacity for growth, or his curiosity, or his respect for his material. They can't take him deeper into a play or a novel, or point forward to new reading, or make him care for truth.

### Alister

In his first year Alister had written on Robert Frost. For his long essay in the third year he wanted to go back to Frost and compare him with one of his English contemporaries. He chose Edward Thomas because of his close friendship with Frost. Having explored first Frost's poems, then Thomas's, he saw that his knowledge of the one was incomplete without knowledge of the other. In his first chapter he called Frost an interpreter and Thomas a recorder. He quoted Frost's poem 'Iris by Night' and a letter of Edward Thomas's describing a rainbow that he had seen with Frost. Whereas Thomas in his letter tells Eleanor Farjeon that it was 'too much of a pure rainbow' for any painter to 'interfere with it', Frost in his poem does 'interfere' – neither the rainbow nor the writer nor his companion is as important as the idea of friendship:

> And we stood in it softly circled round
> From all division time or foe can bring
> In a relation of elected friends.

Frost, from his observations, is prompted to consider further ideas; while Thomas seems to be bound up in ordering his perceptions and experiences of the rainbow.

As Alister found out more about Edward Thomas, this distinction no longer satisfied him. He asked, 'Yet is this the whole truth about the difference between the two men?' He came to this conclusion: 'The end that Thomas found in nature is as creative as Frost's beginning. . . . Frost draws his strength from nature – the strength to see clearly and widely, to comment wisely. Thomas finds his strength *in* nature – the strength to live at peace with himself.' He was able to make this general statement because his knowledge of Edward Thomas and of Frost had been built up poem by poem; he had learned to move out, gradually, from what he knew and understood. He had literally 'wandered with' the poems (as Keats advised) in the country round Steep in Hampshire where Edward Thomas had lived.

Once a student will admit to doubts, there is the beginning of growth.

### Fiona

> I saw before I had well finished
> All suddenly mount
> And scatter wheeling in great broken rings
> Upon their clamorous wings.

Here there can be no argument about the underlying meaning; this is simply beautiful description. One can hear the bursting, beating sound of swans disturbed.

Later in the poem Yeats uses the swans to mark the passage of time, and of the years of his life. They have become a symbol of immutability:

> Unwearied still . . .
> Their hearts have not grown old.

I wonder whether, in the last verse, the swan is taking on a deeper symbolism for Yeats.

Among what rushes will they build,
By what lake's edge or pool
Delight men's eyes when I awake some day
To find they have flown away?

Could it be that they symbolize the gift of poetry? In a letter to his wife, thinking of an image in 'Coole and Ballylee, 1931', he says, 'Yesterday I wrote an account of a sudden ascent of a swan – a symbol of inspiration, I think.' Could he be considering, in this last verse, what would happen if he woke and found that inspiration had 'flown away'? Or is this carrying speculation too far?

Whether the answer is yes or no, Fiona is asking questions, and looking for answers in what Yeats himself wrote. Until they have learned to do this students are like Malcolm before he felt the experience of using the magnets on his own. Once they see that the excitement of reading is between themselves and the writer, a critic becomes a third person outside the dialogue – to be challenged or agreed with in the light of their findings. If criticism has not come from this dialogue with the writer and is not their own contribution to understanding, they may as well be content with reading; and we are poor teachers if we have not taught them this before the end of the second year.

Some images in the letter Coleridge wrote to William Sotheby in 1802, soon after his first draught of 'Dejection', may answer Fiona's question and Yeats's comment on 'Coole Park and Ballylee'. In 'The Wild Swans at Coole' the lake mirrors 'a still sky'; but already, where the swans are, the water is 'brimming'. Coleridge at the beginning of his letter speaks of a 'kindling' in 'that state of nascent existence in the Twilight of Imagination, and just on the vestibule of Consciousness', a stirring of 'commotion'. He had in an earlier letter described a 'creation' as 'starting up' in his mind. Now he tells Sotheby that when he wishes to write a poem, instead of its coming upon him uncalled, he has to *beat it up*. The game that rises is 'slow, heavy, laborious, earth-skimming' – 'a metaphysical bustard': not a 'Covey of poetic Partridges, with 'whirring wings of music', or 'wild Ducks *shaping* their rapid flight'. For Yeats, the true symbol of inspiration is the 'sudden thunder of the mounting swan':

All suddenly mount
And scatter wheeling . . .

The brilliant swans, attended always by 'passion or conquest', embody his sense of mounting power, as the mighty fountain of 'Kubla Khan' had done for Coleridge in the 1790's. The 'bell-beat of their wings' about his head, and the 'great broken rings' as they wheel, image the clamorous music and the difficult consummate shaping of a poem – 'Byzantium', for instance.

Fiona knows that she is treading dangerously in her interpretation of Yeats's poem: an image or symbol containing complex meanings is both open-ended and bound by limits that are shadowy or invisible.

### Penni

> The moving waters in their priestlike task
> Of pure ablution round earth's human shores, . . .

In her criticism of Keats's sonnet Penni shares the contents of this image. It has particular meanings for her; and beyond these, other possible meanings. The meanings it had for Keats in this sonnet are bound up with circumstances and feelings in particular places and at particular times, some of them outside the range of her experience and knowledge. The writing of criticism involves both freedom and restraint.

In 1800 Keats set out for Italy in the hope of staving off his death. The ship hit bad weather in the Channel, and he landed on the Dorsetshire coast. 'It was then,' Monckton Milnes says in *The Life and Letters of John Keats*, 'that he composed that sonnet.' On September 28th he wrote to a friend, 'Land and Sea, weakness and decline are great seperators, but death is the great divorcer for ever. When the pang of this thought has passed through my mind, I may say the bitterness of death is passed.'

The sonnet seems to express this longing for a cessation of pain for ever; and the water image gives the effect of eternity. The image of the eternal sea, that from afar off seems to be baptizing the earth, is calm. It is as if, in reaction against the turbulence of his youthful temperament, the knowledge of impending death has turned his thoughts into a calm, almost religious contemplation of his surroundings.

One is given the impression of the earth's being cleansed and purified by the seas; yet Keats is not asking for the impersonal far off steadfastness of the bright star, which sees the water from a distance. He seeks in the water image some way of expressing his longing to be purged of human frailties, and so to become eternal and enduring, whether with his love or in death.

It seems to me that the fear of eternal separation drove Keats to write this sonnet, fear of the solitariness of death. It is not eternal silence that he fears; if he could be with his love for ever, then death would be welcome.

Penni's words, 'It seems to me that . . .' have a tonic effect after the clichés, generalizations, and indefinite 'we'. She believed that her suggestions were valid, but realized that other interpretations are possible, and that she hadn't exhausted the power of Keats's image. When she wrote the essay, she had not read the passage in his earlier letter describing the views over Windermere ('of the most noble tenderness', that 'make one forget the divisions of life'), with his image of the north star 'open lidded and steadfast over the wonders of the great Power'. She didn't know that the sonnet had been written before his journey to Italy, or that in his earliest version, the last line had begun with the phrase, 'Half passionless . . .' Her insight came from her sympathetic penetration of the image, and its truth seems to be confirmed by the radical change Keats made in this last line: 'And so live ever . . .'

In the most illuminating criticism, there is a balance of feeling and thought. If Penni had read beforehand all that Keats's biographers from Monckton Milnes to Robert Gittings have said about the writing of the sonnet, this might have made her think that everything could be explained in these terms, and interfered with her attempt to understand an individual experience in a poem that is under no obligation to lay bare its roots. She can go on to read the letters with biographers at her elbow, and balance her 'felt' interpretation with their scholarship.

When they learn how to use a writer's notebooks, letters, and prefaces as essential sources, records of the process of writing, students reach another growing point. Now they are looking not from outside, through someone else's criticism, but from inside the writer's mind:

> . . . myself with my pleasures and pains, my powers and my experiences, my deserts and my guilt, my shame and sense of beauty, my dangers, hopes, fears and all my fate.[1]

(And yet they are *not* inside a writer's mind; and they need always to learn how much they do not know, how much will never be known.)

### David

Between school and college David had written nothing but occasional letters. This is part of an essay written at the end of his first year. He was twenty-nine.

At the beginning of *Fears in Solitude* Coleridge describes

> A green and silent spot, amid the hills,
> A small and silent dell! O'er stiller place
> No singing skylark ever poised himself.

[1] Hopkins, Commentary on the *Spiritual Exercises* of St. Ignatius Loyola.

H

How could such a man see the smallest detail without making a note of it so that it is plucked, stored, and transplanted in another world, enriched by its time in his memory?

In a conversation with Hazlitt on the walk from Alfoxden to Nether Stowey, recorded in 'My First Acquaintance with Poets', he said that Wordsworth 'was not prone enough to believe in the traditional superstitions of the place.' The curse, the spectre bark, the hermit, which had been planted in his imagination, were all fertilized by his surroundings and by the people he found on his walks.

On another walk from Stowey to Linton, after they had gone the best part of twenty-five miles a thunderstorm came on, and Coleridge ran out bare-headed to enjoy 'the commotion of the elements' in the Valley of the Rocks. It would appear from his observations that he found the severe driving rain, thunder, and fast-moving clouds stirring to his spirit; they lifted his imagination on to a higher plane, causing his ideas to bubble up as if in unison with the physical action around him. This was the very place where only a few months before, in the November of 1797, he had been caught up in a whirlwind – but this time a mental whirlwind – which stirred up the seeds of 'The Wanderings of Cain'. This work was to have been written in conjunction with Wordsworth; but, perhaps because of the reason he had given Hazlitt, Wordsworth was not able to join in his train of thought. Out of the lion came honey, and out of 'Cain' came 'The Ancient Mariner'. No wonder he ran out into the Valley of the Rocks to be in communion with all it offered.

'The scene around was desolate; as far as the eye could reach it was desolate; the bare rocks faced each other, and left a long and wide interval of thin white sand. . . . Never morning lark had poised himself over this desert . . .'

Dorothy Wordsworth wrote in her Journal for August 31st, 1800, 'At 11 o'clock Coleridge came . . . He came over Helvellyn . . . Talked much about the mountains.'

This is not to be wondered at from a man who was used to the West country hills. Even a layman like myself cannot help being inspired by the grandeur of these mountains; and Coleridge threw himself among them as if longing to commune with them as people. He described in a letter to Sir Humphrey Davy how sheltering under some rocks on Carrock he had worshipped the 'eternal link of energy' in a thunderstorm. After the storm, the rain had made the mountains more distinct. (I have seen this in areas of downland after a storm has swept clouds away.)

'The darkness vanished, as if by enchantment-: far off, to the South the mountains of Glaramara & Great Gavel, and their Family appeared distinct, in deepest, sablest *Blue*!' This is like a Constable.

Through these letters we are brought into contact with Coleridge as a man. I no longer think of him as a name, but try to understand him as I try to understand my neighbours and contemporaries.

## *Valerie*

Valerie wrote on Coleridge in her second year:

His life abounded in exercise. One of his most exciting experiences, which shows me the dexterity of his body, mind, and senses is his solitary climb described in a journal letter (transcribed by Sara Hutchinson) about a tour in the Lake country. He found his way down by a succession of drops from one ledge to another. He became aware of the crags that towered above him and the racing clouds; and praised God for the powers of wit and reason, 'which remaining, no danger can overpower us'. On another day he paused in a sheepfold to call out the names of his friends and hear the echoes. This shows him to have been intensely human – if an extraordinary human being. It amuses me and gives me pleasure.

Accounts in his letters of his children playing express vigorous enthusiasm for their physical freedom and energy, and show his joy as a father: 'Hartley is a Spirit dancing on an aspen leaf . . .', 'he moves, he lives, he finds impulses from within & from without–. . . . He looks at the clouds, the mountains, the living Beings of the Earth, & vaults & jubilates!'

Although they are so much part of nature he sees them responding to impulses from within as well as from without. The interplay of these two sources was uppermost in his mind for most of his life.

> Ah! from the soul itself must issue forth
> A light, a glory, a fair luminous cloud
> Enveloping the Earth–

I think he felt that all meaning came from a reality beyond physical life. There was an absolute truth that it was possible to discover. He yearned for a union in personal relationships, but was gradually disillusioned by his experience. Humphrey House says that he is an example of the paradox 'that in proportion as the desire is strong to be passionately united in all things to somebody else, so must the recognition grow, in area after area of experience, that in the last resort such union is impossible.' He sought to discover this union in his poetic experience, and this passage from *Anima Poetae* shows that he came near to finding it through a projection of himself into nature:

'In looking at objects of Nature while I am thinking, as at yonder moon dim-glimmering through the dewy window-pane, I seem rather to be seeking, as it were *asking* for, a symbolical language for something within me that already and for ever exists, than observing anything new.'

In everyday living, the awareness of his sympathy with such objects forced him to see that this union could be truly felt only when he was alone. In the haunting mystery of the relationship between Christabel and Geraldine, in Geraldine's origin and the strange part she has no choice but to play, and in her association with Christabel's father, I feel that he is grappling with the reality that flows beneath the surface of domestic life and human relationships. The ghastly experiences of the Ancient Mariner, with the intervention and influence of the supernatural, show him expressing his grief at human imperfections by creating spirits that are ideal.

Although when he wrote 'Dejection' he felt that he had lost his creative power, in the symbolism of that poem he still reaches for the same romantic vision and absolute truth as before, 'A light, a glory. . .'. The beautiful image of the glory seems to be the perfect expression of his innermost thought; and the dejection in this poem seems to be the greatest of his sufferings because, being spiritual, it was the deepest torment.

For all his unquiet, his questioning, and disillusionment, he still felt a reverence for life. The Ancient Mariner blessed the water-snakes and so the power of the polar spirit began to slacken. He had realized that the pulse of life was something to be blessed—endless, inexhaustible life.

In a sonnet to Sara Hutchinson, Coleridge expresses his love in the image of a fountain that

'. . . fills and changes all,
Like vernal waters springing up through snow . . .'

The 'mighty fountain' of Xanadu comes from a gigantic volcano. Rocks are being hurled by its force, just like grain threshed in the shattering confusion of an explosion. The words 'ceaseless', 'breathing', 'once and ever', and 'momently' tie together the mystery and the quality of being 'measureless to man'; and finally burst into the fact that it is a sacred river. The breathing of the earth seems to me to be like a breaking out of the darkness of the womb, or the final wrench from the paralysing arms of disease into a new and better spiritual life.

Coleridge is like a fountain. Jets of feeling rise in his poems. They are not undisciplined; they fall in beautiful cadences, with the light playing on the water, and the shadow creating a second fountain of thought.

# [ ii ] Organization of an English course

English course work has to be open, in some measure, to the changing experience of the students. The most satisfying and useful work may begin with a chance happening. Something seen, heard, or learned for the first time can make a piece of writing ring true. In the November of his second year, George a student in the main English group, watched starlings flying over the park before roosting; and remembered an entry in the first volume of Coleridge's *Notebooks*, that he had read the year before. He looked it up.

'Nov. 27. Wed: Starlings in vast flights drove along like smoke, mist, or any thing misty [without] volition – now a circular area inclined [in an] arc – now a globe – [now from a complete orb into an] elipse & oblong – now a balloon with the [car suspend]ed, now a concaved [sem]icircle & [still] it expands & condenses, some [moments] glimmering and shivering, dim & shadowy, now thickening, deepening, blackening! –'

This was an exact description of what he had just seen. He decided to write his long essay in the summer term on details of the English countryside recorded by Gilbert White of Selborne, Cobbett, Bewick, Constable, Coleridge, and Dorothy Wordsworth. He took Gilbert White because he was living in Hampshire at the time, and Dorothy Wordsworth because her Alfoxden Journal overlaps with Coleridge's Quantock poems. He spent some time in the summer in Constable's part of Suffolk. Bewick's wood-engravings and *Memoir* were new to him, but he became an enthusiast and bought a copy of the Dover *1800 Woodcuts by Thomas Bewick and his School*, which has the engravings from all Bewick's more important books.

In his essay he was linking writers with a painter and an engraver. He choose his own material, as he would have to when he began to teach; and it was material that he could use with junior children. Now, after eighteen months' voluntary service in Malawi, he is teaching in a Hampshire village school, and can look for himself at birds, animals, trees, people, and compare them with what Gilbert White and Cobbett saw in the eighteenth and early nineteenth centuries.

Within the very broad outlines of the syllabus approved by Bristol University, a tutor is free to decide which writers have most to give to a particular group of students: something he cannot know before the course has begun.

The work is assessed by the college and an external examiner. Until this last year, when some students began to read for the B. Ed. degree, we had no examinations. Students submit all the work they have done on the course and, if they wish, their independent writing. More weight is given to the long essay and the second part of the course work than to the first part.

The writing that follows is by four students – Hilary, Paul, Sue, Joy – in the same group as Alister, Anne, Carolyn, David, and George.

We met once a week for seminars lasting a whole morning – with an extra hour and a half for tutorials in the second year. In the third year there were two morning sessions, so that each student had five or six short tutorials in which to discuss his long essay.

For the first year we worked as one group; after that in two groups of ten. Most people felt more at ease and talked more freely in the smaller groups. In the second year, when we had the extra time for tutorials, I taught one group and a colleague the other; in the third, two of us shared the work, taking the half groups in alternate sessions, or all twenty students together. From time to time throughout the course other tutors took two or three seminars at a stretch; and colleagues from different departments came to speak about music – the *War Requiem* or Britten's settings of Donne, or on what philosophy is about. Teachers from Bristol, Wiltshire, and Oxfordshire schools talked with us about their children's writing and reading, and the experiences of immigrant children. I was in touch with this group for three years, and learned the value of continuity within variety.

When a student is truly involved in work with children, a story or a poem is like a seed-case whose seeds are germinating and sprouting. (There is enough in *Sir Gawain and the Green Knight* for them to explore for weeks on end.) The germinating should begin in his own reading, beforehand. The fact that Donne possessed a Titian,[1] for instance, raises all kinds of questions. For particularly rich and complex material – the medieval and renaissance background to *Dr Faustus*, or the poems of Yeats – our Librarian let us have a bay where books and pictures could be left for two or three weeks so that everyone in the group could browse there in an unhurried way.

Their first year talks and third year long essays were probably the most useful parts of the course work prepared by the students. In the talk, they were learning, and communicating what they had learned. They chose the subjects from a list of suggestions, or added their own suggestions. I wanted them to look at some of the writing and painting (of Ibsen, Baudelaire, Cézanne, Kafka, Brecht, Camus, Orwell, Picasso) that lay behind the contemporary writers they were reading; and I hoped that, as we went along, a network of parallels and contrasts would begin to form in our minds.

---

[1] Helen Gardner, *The Elegies and the Songs and Sonnets of John Donne*, Oxford University Press.

# [ iii ] Reading and Writing

*Hilary*

Hilary, in the second half of her course, wrote a series of twenty-five poems. We had been reading Beckett and Eliot in the term before. In the summer vacation at the end of the second year she began to read for her long essay. Writing it in the autumn, she tried to bring her thoughts and reading into perspective. The poems and essay overlapped; they were parts of the same process of digesting experience.

In the poems, she was trying to express a state of mind; she had begun to doubt things that she had always taken for granted:

> I am not in a condition to say or be anything definite.
>
> Nomad born, with three parts
> of a riddle . . .

In one it seems as if the answer might come through imagination, 'the rain of a deep longing' – though this might be 'the illusion of a poem'; in another, through the common chords in our experience. She is looking for signs of a nourishing hope, permanence, and order; making some kind of bridge between George Herbert or Julian of Norwich, and her own uncertainty.

My first joy at being articulate was followed by doubt as to whether the words were worth the paper they were written on; and so I wrote another poem – to restore confidence, I suppose. This lack of confidence, which lives with me through everything I do, may partly explain why I write. Writing may be an escape from myself and the world outside: I can escape into the enjoyment of working on a poem about problems bigger than the ones that are troubling me at the time. The emotional energy generated by these smaller problems gives rise to writing of a more impersonal nature – though there are some subjects that one cannot write about without first using the medium self-indulgently. Whatever the reason, I must write.

I usually have ideas waiting. I can't work in silence. Some poems come easily, with few alterations; others change form, and take a long time to finish. It becomes almost an obsession to finish a poem.

Many poems come from chance happenings. 'Night-music' came when I had acute toothache. I was standing at a bus stop; gusts of wind sounded in the trees across the road, then they struck me. Before writing, I had seen some cracked, rotting violins hanging in a dusty cupboard as if they were old brushes; there is nothing more tragic or pathetic than a cracked violin. This violin is an Aeolian Harp. The image

> A cloud's old jaws, pearl-lit,
> Eagerly devour the moon . . .

came from what I saw a few nights later: the full moon disappearing into clouds shaped like jaws. The savage image stayed in my mind. The last verse shows my preoccupation with the void at the time. In the prose notes working out the poem, I wrote: 'Thoughts have all been expressed; only images remain to express themselves.'

NIGHT-MUSIC
A cracked violin hanging
in black shapes of trees
creaks and trills the night;
here at least I have
a slight warning
of what may happen to me,
but nowhere else.

A cloud's old jaws, pearl-lit,
eagerly devour the moon;
dead, to be born again
with new beauty.
But who sees the moon's pain
While she waits for re-birth?

Painting an empty night
with images shrouding cruelty.
What images are there
left to man when
the overshadowing image is life
painted on empty time
in a dream by an eager hand
called Imagination?

I was concerned with the problem of perceiving and communicating reality; and influenced by Beckett's thought. Reality is the artist's insoluble problem.

I painted the night with images, not knowing the full meaning behind them. I only knew that it was elemental and cruel: but was I imposing this upon it? What was the reality behind the night, if there was no one there to perceive it? It seems to me that we perceive reality in images, that we do not get any nearer to reality than an image of it. Imagination, man's most precious and most damning gift, imposes a false reality upon life.

I am conscious of influences: contemporary poets such as Prévert (I have taken his sun-flower and turned it into a dandelion), and the mystical writings of St. John of the Cross, St. Teresa of Avila, and the Upanishads. Biblical phrases echo through my mind. The clear shadow of T. S. Eliot can be seen over all the poems. The metaphysicals, especially Donne, are important to me; I should like all my first lines to be dynamic and shattering, like his. If I write of thorns, I have in mind Sutherland's hanging forms, or the knotted forms of his trees.

In 'The Tyranny of Time', I wanted to show man trapped in time: the war on time is a war against our nature as finite, temporal beings. I could find only

one way that was free. Imagination was the eye that could see the experience
of the mystics outside time:

> ... On a black soft hillock
> clothed in nightmass
> relieved by heaven's sparks,
> I understood that – unmarked
> by the oppressive shadow.

> Nature feeding from the earth
> marks its gradual autumnal change
> when it wills.
> It can only glimpse
> the edge of the shadow.

> The night-fires free from earth,
> the stars singing of freedom,
> have seen Julian in Norwich
> wearing love, outside time;
> and another reaching the real destination,
> timeless and undesiring.

'Towards Gabo' was written after I had seen pictures of Gabo's constructions, and heard him being interviewed on the radio. I was enthralled by his
idea of images in space and time. Several poems harp on this theme of three-
dimensional existence:

> Delicate wires join one to all.
> So we are held blindly
> to lovers, friends, and strangers.

TOWARDS GABO

> Write these words
> across the rich blue sky
> at evening, in scarlet interwoven silk;
> or carve them deep into the skin
> of underground caverns,
> where shadows may play around them
> chasing the sun ceaselessly
> while the sun has breath to run.
> Here they stay dead,
> stranded in paperdimension
> (though Herbert could order them,
> flying across your vision)
> until your eyes summon them
> to life in your mind.

> Have you allowed them life?
> Then watch them grow
> Out of their one dimension
> through the length of your brain

to join the breadth of all thought.
See them rounded now,
fully formed in the tensions
of time and space.
Once your thoughts join
with mine on this paper,
we have no need to struggle
with matter to create.
The thoughts are suspended
in time as they are thought;
on slim nylon threads
they spin through space
and eternity. Once thought,
they are indestructible.
Another will be scarred by them
when they are still living,
and we dead.

See where the forces
touch and cross in space,
leaving each other in peace.
See the web of perfection,
woven to say a different word
in each uncounted direction.
Still, yet ever-moving
nylon threads, shimmering
through space in time.
A complete art
built on tension-form.
Lines of force combining
in mutual respect, losing
their identity for art.
When even their creator
has not courage enough
to follow the example
he has created.

We had read *A Passage to India* in the first year. The image in
this last poem of Hilary's:

> . . . carve them deep into the skin
> of underground caverns,
> where shadows may play around them
> chasing the sun ceaselessly
> while the sun has breath to run.

may have come from E. M. Forster's Marabar Caves: 'A mirror
inlaid with lovely colours . . . exquisite nebulae . . . all the evane-
scent life of the granite . . . skin . . . smoother than windless

water . . .' If it was Forster's to begin with, this image has behaved exactly as Hilary describes in her poem – taken on independent life in a different context. In the Caves, 'sounds did not echo or thoughts develop'. In Hilary's poem, a form made by Gabo is an image of the echoing, changing life that words may live.

Her image in 'Night-music',

> A cloud's old jaws, pearl-lit,
> eagerly devour the moon,

has a power that seems to be independent of her present strength as a writer. For the fraction of a minute, light floods the edges of the cloud. Hidden in the cloud, the moon waits to be born again. The predatory cloud drifts; the indestructible moon glides on its course. This could be an image of the effect on one another of the supernatural and the human; or of death and re-birth. Or again, the jaws eager to devour the moon are like man's old greed for union with infinity, beauty, immortality, or whatever unattainable and indestructible thing he wants to make part of himself and be replenished by. It may be another instance of the kind Sir Kenneth Clark described (mentioned on page 67 in connection with a child's image of a bear's claws 'on the mouth of an unknown animal'), that continues to act as a living symbol because it speaks to part of the mind that doesn't change with time. It says

> . . . a different word
> in each uncounted direction.

This may be why Hilary, writing on this poem, says that 'images remain', to 'express themselves'.

### Paul

I write because I enjoy writing. I like the sounds of words and phrases; and sometimes, perhaps, the sound becomes more important than the sense, though I try to avoid this. The inspiration (if you can call it this) may come from a piece of music, or a dusty city; but this only provides the spark: the writing depends on what is already in my mind.

#### THOUGHTS WITH SNOW

> Winding its apparitions into my eyes,
> turning my mind with re-appearing images,
> the snow, wind-torn fragments of white birds,
> bandages the earth's encrusted wounds
> and unwraps mine.

A boy bowed in an empty bus shelter
watches the four-wheeled world in motion;
having missed the last chance, he must walk
down the coldness of unknown foot-paths.

Joy, like sorrow, is not remembered in degrees,
because the ultimate is unattainable.
The day, the place, where your feet were bleeding,
are chipped in the frozen pavings;
the rest is buried.

No-one bows in the empty bus shelter;
look again: there is only snow and the wind
prowling under the bench, mauling the used tickets,
and revolving passing shadows.

Attempting explanations destroys and disillusions,
like grasping frost-iced cobwebs from a hedge.
A phrase has added and subtracted meaning
in sympathetic hearts, but otherwise must be
a trick of intellectuals.

Nothing exists in a non-existent bus shelter.
There is only the snow, drifting, banking, burying.
Don't look; it is unnecessary, and tomorrow
perhaps the sun will shine.

Snow means many things to many people. It turned my mind to other times when it was snowing, and to what was happening then. The snow inspired the remembering described in the poem. I saw a boy in a bus shelter once, when I was passing in a car. I must have seen him for only two seconds, but the picture has remained. He was freer than I was (I am certain he was not waiting for a bus); and in a way, he symbolizes freedom. For most people complete freedom is unattainable; and if they had it, they could not live with it for more than a few hours. At some time or other they see it, but the sacrifice of comfort (physical and mental) is so great that they pass it by until it no longer exists. It fades like something they have seen on a journey. At a later stage, in similar circumstances, the memory throws up the image again; but they can no longer remember the significance, and as the circumstances fade, so does the memory – like the melting of snow in the sun.

The third verse contains independent memories. It is impossible to remember how much sadness or pain you felt on a certain occasion. You cannot say, 'It hurt 80%.'

When I wrote the poem, I longed to change places with the boy in the shelter – although I would probably not have enjoyed this freedom for long.

The images in the first verse of 'Thoughts with Snow' (of apparitions, a globe that fills with snow when you turn it, birds' feathers, bandages) suggest a complete experience of memory and of snow. The other verses are less satisfying and less clear – though their unclearness seems to have come from fullness rather than emptiness. A number of thoughts and feelings have taken shape and rhythm in images, but Paul hasn't said enough to connect them: his notes do this. I prefer the poem as it is to the poem it would have been if he had made an effort to fill in the gaps.

This may in time become the 'unclearness' of writing whose meaning unfolds itself gradually. In his long essay he came to grips with writing of this kind: complex, ironic, concentrating its meanings in beautifully 'organized' forms.

## The Poetry of Robert Lowell
### The introduction and the last section

With every new generation, man has developed a more efficient means of destroying himself; and in this century he has taken the longest stride in the shortest time. His reaction to his behaviour in two world wars has been shock, outrage, almost disbelief; but he cannot live in a prolonged state of anguish, and gradually these feelings have been tempered to a bearable disgust and a morbid curiosity about the future. This fearful curiosity is probably more acute now than it has ever been: there is the possibility of an accidental holocaust as the man-machine components of defence systems grow more complex. For me, no writer expresses the feeling of horror so well as Robert Lowell. He paints his world in greys, blacks, and whites; and strews his landscapes with sewers, smoke, and diseases, over which there hangs a sky filled with eternal winter. It is a cruel world, a world from which love and beauty, as these were understood before, have vanished.

### Time and Redemption

'In a poem you don't try to give the reader distress and disorder: you want to give him something well made and organized, with loveliness to it.' (Lowell in conversation with John Gale, the *Observer*, 12th March 1967.)

There seem to be two dominant themes in *For The Union Dead*, Lowell's most recent volume of poems. Again he writes about the flux of time, and now he expands this theme. He acknowledges the essential aloneness in which man exists, and examines his internal conflicts and complexities in an external complex society.

Many of the poems are written in retrospect. They express sympathy and, on occasion, guilt. He believes that he has misjudged his father; and, having reached middle age himself, asks his forgiveness. In 'Alfred Corning Clark', he is reminded by an obituary of an old school friend who differed from him in his attitude to life. Life presents a series of lessons, and each man reacts individually to them, expecting no help. Lowell believes that there can

be sympathy, because the problems are shared. 'The Mouth of the Hudson'
reveals sympathy not for any particular people he has known, but for one
man and all men: one man on the river bank in the 'Chemical air' and the
'sulphur-yellow sun', unable to understand his own situation, and confused
by the realities with which he is confronted.

> He cannot discover Americas by counting
> the chains of condemned freight trains
> from thirty states. They jolt and jar
> and junk in the siding below him.
> He has trouble with his balance.

Ice, 'Like the blank sides of a jig-saw puzzle,
> The ice ticks seaward like a clock.

He may or may not see the other side; the implication points to a negative
answer.

There are several beautiful, delicately expressed love poems, – love,
perhaps, being man's saving grace, in view of his ultimate failure.

The first poem in the book establishes the mood – incorporating sympathy,
a sense of loss, memory, and the recognition of isolation. Lowell is speaking
to a woman. The language is simple and powerful.

> It was a Maine lobster town –
> each morning boatloads of hands
> pushed off for granite
> quarries on the islands . . .
>
> . . . below us the sea lapped
> the little raw match-stick
> masses of a weir,
> where the fish for bait were trapped.

The rock is painted by memory until it seems

> the color
> of iris, rotting and turning purpler.

For most people, this would be sufficient. But Lowell knows that all the time
in reality, there was no colour except

> the usual gray rock
> turning the usual green
> when drenched by the sea.

He appreciates and surmounts the natural desire to romanticize memories; and
suggests that it would be more honest and nearer to reality if man could
remember exactly, and live with the true memory instead of the beautiful
versions he creates. The relentless passing of time is expressed in the verse,

> The sea drenched the rock
> at our feet all day,
> and kept turning away
> flake after flake.

The woman dreamed that she was a mermaid,

> ... trying to pull
> off the barnacles ...

as if in a physical attempt to break the barrier of time, prevent change, and return to the memory: an attempt that must be futile. Both she and Lowell wished at the time to return; but now he understands that they and the place have changed, and that reality would shatter memory. Even as they existed within the moment, the moment was changing and passing – perhaps while they were already beginning to form the memory rather than remember the actual happening. The climax is compressed:

> In the end,
> the water was too cold for us.

Lowell would not wish to escape the reality of change. In 'The Old Flame' and 'Returning', he assesses familiar places in relation to his changed stature.

> Remember our list of birds?
> One morning last summer, I drove
> by our house in Maine.

Modernization and mechanization have come.

> Everything's changed for the best-

Lowell says; but from the lines that follow –

> how quivering and fierce we were,
> there snow-bound together ...

it is clear that even if he does not imply the opposite this statement is not intended to be taken as literal truth. There is no returning from the present to the past. Future change was already 'groaning up hill' like the plough,

> a red light, then a blue,
> as it tossed off the snow
> to the side of the road.

In 'Returning', he re-lives memories of childhood. The town is first seen as it is in reality:

> Nothing is deader than this small town main street ...

But he remembers it brighter and clearer than this, as a child, unable to make comparisons and incapable of large perspectives, would once have seen it. Finally, reality returns: although memory still intrudes to remind him of the past, he is alone with the realization that he has outgrown the town.

In 'The Lesson', he captures the feeling of permanence one has in childhood. I believe that a basic aim of artists – and possibly of other men – is to regain the simple and unprejudiced view-point of a child and to combine this with adult experience: simplicity and openness, with understanding and compassion. Lowell has discovered the permanence of repetition. Although a man may consider himself to be unique, in this respect he is part of a recurring pattern.

> The barberry berry sticks on the small hedge,
> cold slits the same crease in the finger,
> the same thorn hurts. The leaf repeats the lesson.

Now that he is forty-five, he remembers his father at the same age. Gone is the scathing criticism: his father never succeeded, but Lowell realizes that no one ever can. In 'Middle Age', he follows his father's footsteps by a different route:

> You never climbed
> Mount Zion, yet left
> dinosaur
> death-steps on the crust,
> where I must walk.

In 'Those Before Us' (the title contains a double meaning), he accepts the fact that others whom he criticized in the past had tried to live as he is doing now.

In his final poem, 'For the Union Dead', he accepts the passing of time. Boston Aquarium is derelict and forgotten, standing in a 'Sahara of snow'. Three statements are sufficient to establish this:

> Its broken windows are boarded.
> The bronze weather vane cod has lost half its scales.
> The airy tanks are dry.

He used to visit it as a child; his nose 'crawled like a snail on the glass' – the simile suggesting that this is not merely a place he once visited, but a part of his life. Now the land is being used for redevelopment: 'yellow dinosaur steamshovels' ('dinosaur' suggesting a regressive rather than a progressive step in relation to reality) are gouging an 'underworld garage' for 'giant finned cars'. The dead mechanical cars are replacing the living, real fish. Metal girders face the statue of Colonel Shaw, whose monument

> sticks like a fish-bone
> in the city's throat.

The statue is a redundant piece of the past. Life (in the full sense of the word) is dead. The modern Bostonians, compared with the early New Englanders, are spiritual aliens, concerned only with material improvement. Whereas Lowell's earlier comments were made in disgust, anger, and perhaps incredulity, here is the slow, mature awareness that man's progress is very slow. He must make all the mistakes of previous generations before he can take even a little step forward. He does not want reality, and his ability to romanticize the past helps him to convince himself of his uniqueness, and sets his mind at rest.

The stone statues of the abstract Union Soldier
grow slimmer and younger each year –
wasp-wasted, they doze over muskets
and muse through their side-burns . . .

He is still concerned about the wrong things – for example, the conquest of
space, rather than racial integration. Colonel Shaw has 'an angry wren-like
vigilance';

> he rejoices in man's lovely
> peculiar power to choose life and die.

*For the Union Dead* is the most recent of Lowell's works to be published in
this country. He is concerned in it with the unnaturalness that man has come
to regard as natural, the spiritually abnormal that is materially normal. He
begins with an enlightened, uncompromising attitude; and this is gradually modified, because he is realistic enough to know that our understanding
of reality – if this is ever likely to come about – will come very slowly. In the
meantime, we must compromise and find redemption through compassion,
sympathy, and love.

> Two walking cobwebs, almost bodiless,
> crossed paths here once, kept house, and lay in beds.
> Your fingertips once touched my fingertips
> and set us tingling through a thousand threads.
> Poor pulsing Fête Champêtre! The summer slips
> between our fingers into nothingness.

## Sue

I started writing when I came back from Norfolk – after an intense
experience and a situation, place, and time that I wanted to recapture. I hoped
by doing so to order my experience. I saw that the prose I was writing contained images: I was not able to express the experience in any other way than
by images.

Next day I began writing in verse, and I found that the images I had
already used were recurring and were prompting others. I wrote down
phrases and images, and realized that I had the material for three poems.
Suddenly I saw a shape in one of them: I had the three central verses ready
and I added a beginning and an ending. The other two I left in their pencilled
form, except that when I was working them out in ink I reconsidered
individual words and phrases.

The poems are highly personal. I felt impelled to write them because my
feelings were so strong. You come to Norfolk: a scene into which you
project some thought of yours that has been in your mind before though
perhaps not in that particular form – something dormant that comes up into
something actual. More recently I have written to straighten out thoughts
which are forming and whirling in my mind. If there is a problem, I want to
clarify it: the poem is a working out of thoughts, though perhaps they are not
'thoughts' when I begin to write – when it's finished it's not always what I
expected.

I

It now seems more natural to work out ideas in a poem than in prose. Perhaps this is because most of them come in images. I've noticed that an image often occurs in connection with a particular thought and that I explore it as I write: its components seem to relate to the components of the subject. Suddenly the images are in my mind and I know that I have something to write about.

I used to re-shape poems. But your feeling may not have stayed the same, so that if you alter a poem its character may change. For this reason I don't like altering – though you may get an extension or a maturing of the thought with the passing of time. You are less intensely involved in the poem – that is, in the writing of it; although still, of course, involved in the experience. Perhaps you can find more truth.

It's often hard to resist putting in a word for its own quality. I find that there are some words that I like for their sounds or shapes and sometimes I wonder whether they convey anything real. English words can be magical on their own, and as Samuel Beckett found, they may obscure meaning because of their evocative quality.

I usually write late at night. I imagine that the experience has been fomenting in my mind, so that it is not a purely haphazard process.

Recently I have been more and more dissatisfied with what I write. It seems trivial, like playing a game. I am conscious of influences – Elizabeth Jennings, Lawrence Durrell, for instance. This worries me but I suppose it is inevitable. I should like to be able to achieve simplicity and truth, and I hate to feel that my work is at all pretentious. What I write now doesn't represent any kind of fruition; it will not, I hope, be anything like what I may write later on; but it is a beginning, a searching for the way.

SUMMER POEMS

I

Can I capture a love so transient in a line?
The essence of time in an image?
Butterfly wing beauty, subtle and soft,
like water held in cupped hands,
pure and clear, seemingly deep, shallow reality.
Drop by drop it slipped out of our grasp,
unseen, unnoticed until drained away.
The unheeding acuteness of youth
caught and tasted and lost all in one summer.

II

I hear the lone trumpet calling on the sea shore,
on the wide white sand to the quiet mother-of-pearl sea.
Sound delicate as filagree, sculptured as ice,
like some icicle needle in the moonlight,
solitary and proud in its dignity.
Expecting no reply from the empty wave,

calling only to the kindred sea-bird in the vast sky
its aching lost message.
I hear in those lyrical notes
echo of calm dunes and sea-bird solitariness,
lunar serenity and sun-separateness.


## ON HENRY VAUGHAN'S POEM 'THE WATER-FALL'

I read your poem and I touch your mind.
I share a thought of yours and find
that rhyme, which is foreign to me,
is over-mastering my senses and nerves,
leading me to the edge of your river;
to a presumptuous communion feast,
to a heady wine and tantalizing bread.
I would believe I could partake with you
in the moment of inception, of discovery,
of that perfect image in a sensitive mind.
Man's life is like water in a stream, you say;
and I, confident, step to the brink of the falls
to assert my kinship with the image,
and recognition of my own method of portrayal.
But the roar of falling water covers my pride,
to remind me of the facile influence
your rhymes had on my pliant mind.
And I step back from the water-fall edge,
lest I drown.


## ARMOUR

I have seen the living death of a tree.
A child killed it with his name and a knife.
He skinned off the armour of bark
and laid open the tender sap to the salt air.
If I take off your armour I will kill you, too.
I will kill you as surely and as innocently as a child.


Sue and Joy in their long essays, printed here in shortened form, came to similar conclusions.

Sue's essay grew out of her writing. She saw that once a poem had been shared, it had come to hold other people's experiences as well as hers.

She asks questions that lead to further questions; and reaches her conclusions after examining individual passages. For instance, in her first section she looks at the part played by an image in one of her own poems to illustrate a definition found in her reading, and compares images from 'Burnt Norton' and a poem by Cavafy to test the truth of the statement that imagery can express what would otherwise be inexpressible.

Of the material she uses, Pound, Cavafy, O'Casey, and the early Irish poems she had read on her own; the medieval lyrics, Border ballads, Coleridge, Keats's letters, Eliot, and Yeats as part of the course work. She had written on 'Leda and the Swan', Eliot's images of water in the 'Quartets', Spender's 'Seascape', and Keats's sense of identity. Hopkins's poem 'Spring and Fall' made a deep impression on her.

### Sue

### The image in poetry

There have been times in my life when a scene, a person, or a feeling has touched me deeply, and I have tried to contain it, using the form of a poem. I eventually realized that my thoughts were being expressed in images, and it seemed to me that my own primitive use of the image might cause me to appreciate more easily the masterly use of it by great poets. It also occurred to me that imagery must be one of the basic elements of poetry if I, an absolute beginner, instinctively used it. I began to read about imagery. I had thought of it as an isolated feature of my own work, and now I saw that it was the essence of poetry. The more I read, the more complex and exciting imagery seemed to be, and the more elusive.

Ezra Pound has a poem whose imagery, form, and expression are the most satisfying I know.

> Be in me as the eternal mood
>         of the bleak wind, and not
> As transient things are –
>         gaiety of flowers
> Have in me the strong loneliness
>         of sunless cliffs
> And of grey waters.
>         Let the gods speak softly of us
> In days hereafter,
>         The shadowy flowers of Orcus
> Remember thee.

This poem stands in itself as cold letters, but there is something in it that sets up a feeling of harmony between myself and the words. I think this feeling is given by the images of wind, cliffs, and waters; but the attempt to pinpoint its impact is almost futile. How it is done, the mind is not aware of at the time. It is afterwards that I find myself asking questions. If I presume to write poetry, an awareness of what it is and how it works may help me to write better. Yet such a search seems to lead to a barrier, for poetry is not a science, nor are images interlocking atoms in a structure.

The danger with a search of this kind is that you might be led to declare blindly, 'This is what an image is'; and believe that the application of the formula would solve every problem – reducing the art to a craft. I do not believe that this will happen. I hope to find some answer to the question, 'What use is poetry to us?' – a common one in this scientifically minded age where usefulness is the criterion of worth. I know that poetry supplies me with something. In the search I may discover what areas in the human personality it touches, and whether it can reach everyone. I want to know how imagery works; to know why Ezra Pound's poem has such an effect on me.

I

## Communication and the image

I have asked the question, 'Why?' I am asking, in effect, 'What does imagery seek to do, and how does it do it?'

The problem comes to me in an image. The essence of a poem is the skeleton; and the poetic form, and surface and under-surface meanings are its body. When I have probed the outer realities, I hope to arrive at some inner reality, related to them and yet separate.

The difficulty I have just experienced in laying out this conception satisfactorily, and the fact that I have used an analogy seem to give the key to my question, 'What?' I was seeking to explain something which it was almost impossible to say in literal words – reproducing the abstract by means of the concrete.

The vision of the poet and the vision of the reader are on different planes, and the one can be communicated in terms of the other. The early poets taught the people through songs and myths, making use of the physical world and natural things to convey their thoughts. 'The Old Woman of Beare', an eighth century Irish poem translated by Frank O'Connor, is a lament for the passing of time; the poet even regrets that the suffering caused by the ups and downs of fortune have passed.

> . . . Floodtide!
> Flood or ebb upon the strand?
> What the floodtide brings to you,
> Ebbtide carries from your hand.

> Flood tide
> Ebbtide with the hurrying fall,
> All have reached me, ebb and flow,
> Until now I know them all.

> . . . Happy island of the main
> To you the tide will come again,
> Though to me it comes no more
> Over the blank deserted shore.

Seeing it, I can scarcely say
'Here is such a place,' today
What was water far and wide
Changes with the ebbing tide.

I am sure that the people who listened to this already knew the truths it contains; but they did not realize that they knew, and were not able to put this vague knowledge into communicable form. The poet with his greater skill and understanding did it for them – in his imagery.

If this were all imagery could do, the poet would be merely a spokesman. So far I have discussed the image as a homely tool. Frank Kermode's phrase in *The Romantic Image* – 'a means to truth' – conveys so much more than this. The image may itself be the truth. The abstraction behind its mask is sometimes unformed in the poet's mind. He may use the image in the hope of capturing that truth which, paradoxically, he is using it to express. I believe from my own experience that the image moulds and guides the inchoate mass of partly realized thoughts in your mind, and brings them into meaning for you. Either the thought has not existed as an entity in your mind or else it has existed as the shadowy roots of something which you do not quite understand and certainly could not put into plain words. The image, here, expresses the inexpressible or releases the unknown.

When T. S. Eliot, in Part II of 'Burnt Norton', writes,

Garlic and sapphire in the mud
Clot the bedded axle-tree

his images, which are the outer signs of what he is describing, give a picture and an understanding of what lies behind it. I find that this image yields not one thought but several inter-related thoughts. Eliot wants to say something about war, waste, and time, and their inter-relationship: an undertaking so complex that I do not believe he could have expressed it adequately in words with only literal meanings. He builds an image that shows the results of these things, and so communicates a sense of the things themselves. The whole savour of the idea could not have been conveyed by other means; something would have been left out, and this would probably have been the elusive relationship between these things. By using images describing the aftermath of war, waste, and time, he can be sure that the something he could not wholly express has been included in his poem, although in a shadowy way. There are conceptions such as time, space, existence, emotion, death, on which our comprehension stumbles. These are the very conceptions that show most complexity in their natures. They are the themes that poets are grappling with when they use imagery to convey what they feel but do not know, whose variety they sense but cannot sum up without losing something.

Imagery avoids this loss of fullness because in its use of pictures it allows the reader's mind to fill in so much background. The fuller the image-picture, the more fully the reader comprehends the essence of the idea lying behind it. C. P. Cavafy's poem 'In the House of the Soul' leaves me with an understanding of certain emotions that I cannot fully explain. I may think that I have not grasped Cavafy's meaning, but I find this understanding again whenever I read the poem in Rae Dalven's translation:

Desires saunter in the House of the Soul –
lovely ladies silken-gowned
and sapphire-crowned.
They command all the halls of the House from the floor
to the depths. In the largest hall –
on nights when their blood is ardent –
they dance and drink with loosened hair.

Outside the halls, pale and shabbily dressed
in the clothes of olden days,
the Virtues pace about and listen in bitterness
to the carousal of the drunken Heterae.
Faces are glued to window panes
and silently, in deep thought they gaze,
at the lights, the jewels, and the flowers of the dance.

This is a more explicit use of imagery than T. S. Eliot's. We know that the Heterae are used as analogies for desires; whereas in the quotation from 'Burnt Norton' we realize that the garlic, the sapphires, the mud, imply something of which they, in their relationship, are part. Yet in both poems it is not so much a question of meaning being caught as of essence being sketched out. The reader makes up the full picture in his mind, as it appears to him to be. So I would modify my supposition that imagery tries to express the inexpressible; this can never be done. Rather, an image gives its atmosphere and feeling and leaves the expressing for the reader to do in his own mind.

In *Poetry and Experience* Archibald Macleish quotes a definition by Lu Chi of the poet's art: the poet is one who 'traps Heaven and Earth in the cage of form'. 'Heaven and Earth' is this almost inexpressible idea, but it is also the unknown element in the poet's mind of which I spoke earlier. The cage is the image, which is not only a trap that prevents the idea from escaping but also a means by which the poet can look at the idea. Once an idea appears in image form, it is comprehensible; it has limits which the image imposes. If the linking of ideas and images in the poet's mind is an unconscious process, the image, not the idea, will dictate these limits of meaning and the lengths to which the idea is taken.

I can explain this best if I illustrate it from my own writing. I suddenly realize that this poem – on 'a sea of ideas lapping and ebbing, swelling and falling' – is about the very thing I have been discussing:

... I have thought I grasped a flower from that garden,
to find it turn to dead leaf in my hand.
The buds are there submerged in that salt water.
I would catch the stars I can form, the fire, and the air;
But always the ripples rouse, and my hand closes on emptiness.

At the back of my mind was a vague idea of some knowledge that I was not able to conceive. Some images came, which by their nature determined the meaning of what I afterwards wrote. The sea image meant that the state of these ideas was never static. It also dictated that the 'buds' should be in salt water, which I saw implied an action on the buds of ideas. I did not know these things when I sat down to write. The images drew out the thoughts. In a sense the poem is not mine: the image dictated it. An image has a life of its own; it can mould your vague conceptions and leave you with a result that says something you could not have said before.

It is inevitable that when one conception is expressed in terms of another it will be changed. A relationship will have developed between the two; so that both – the image, and its essence – are changed into a third conception. This is the germ of the creative process. The image helps the poet to discover something. It may not have been what he set out to seek, but that makes the discovery all the more exciting.

Imagery now seems to be even more complex than I made it out to be when I began. Its existence is not altogether at the command of the poet who brings it into being. But he is the one who conceives it.

2

## Emotion and the image

I now come to the question, 'How?', which I asked at the beginning. It brings me back to the unknown cause of my response to Ezra Pound's poem.

Pound himself in his essay 'A Retrospect' has defined an image as 'that which presents an intellectual and emotional complex in an instant of time.' The key word here is 'complex'. I think it embodies a series of meanings: a unit – perhaps an idea or a picture, one that is not simple or all on one level; a response, which the image elicits. It strikes me as crucial that Pound refers to the complex as intellectual and emotional. The intellect and the emotions both play their part in poetry, for they are both natural parts of man and any undertaking of his is affected by them both. If one or the other predominates then the whole man is not playing his part.

The role of the intellect seems to me to be straightforward. The complex embodies meaning and the reader uses his mind to grasp the sheer physical structure of the image. Similarly on the poet's side the act of writing a poem, of giving ideas form, demands intellect. Perhaps intellect is what Lu Chi meant when he referred to the 'cage of form'.

When I look at the part emotion plays in this complex, the questions multiply instead of decreasing. How does an image make its particular impact? Is it through its own emotional content? Or through the reader's emotional response?

Emotions like love and grief live fiercely in circumstances which to the mind, particularly an outside mind, do not merit their ferocity. In Hopkins's poem 'Spring and Fall', Margaret is shaken by her irrational grief:

> Margaret, are you grieving
> Over Goldengrove unleaving?

The idea that emotion cannot be explained satisfactorily is underlined:

> Sorrow's springs are the same.
> Nor mouth had, no nor mind, expressed
> What heart heard of, ghost guessed:
> It is the blight man was born for,
> It is Margaret you mourn for.

Margaret's experience is something only the heart knows of, and knows without understanding. This sums up for me not only the impossibility of comprehending emotional responses, but also the impossibility of assessing the impact of emotional appeals. If this statement seems to invalidate my essay, then I must, like Hopkins, attempt the impossible. What his poem says of Margaret's grief is true of the relationship between the reader and the image; it can never be wholly explained. This is why I think emotion plays an important part in it.

After reading a poem that has made an impression on you it is difficult to put into words exactly what has happened. This statement from *Sean O'Casey* by David Krause is aimed at the mind; a response from the heart would be out of place and would not help one's understanding: 'The form of *The Plough and the Stars* is more expansive and varied than the conventional form of *The Shadow of a Gunman* because the greater scope and intention make greater demands upon the treatment of the material.' These lines in Stephen Spender's 'Seascape' evoke a quite different response:

> There are some days the happy ocean lies
> Like an unfingered harp, below the land.
> Afternoon gilds all the silent wires
> Into a burning music for the eyes.

Comprehension is joined by a feeling for the scene, and a mood is reproduced in us. This must be what Wordsworth meant by the words (in his second Preface to *Lyrical Ballads*), 'truth . . . . carried alive into the heart by passion' –asserting that it is the heart at which poetry is directed, the illogical, uncontrollable heart. The word 'passion' refers to the deep and vivid response it evokes. The reader not only feels, he 'lives' the words in Stephen Spender's poem: he is made to experience the gentle movement, the sun-coloured surface of the sea.

An emotional response comes forth instantaneously, without being ordered or transmuted. I have noticed that you can convince people with reasoning, but that the conviction is never firmly rooted because it will always be open to further reasoning. But if you touch someone's emotions, he will find this hold harder to disturb because it goes deeper to something unreasoning. The image that gains this deep hold makes itself powerful, sometimes unforgettable. In the Russian film of *Hamlet*, the camera focuses for several minutes on rushing, leaping fire. As I watched this I found all kinds of emotions welling in me – fear, fascination, awe, and a sense of timelessness and time-devouring. These could be rationalized afterwards if I referred them to the theme of the play; but my deep feeling at the time of watching couldn't be rationalized.

Why should the image be able to unloose this reaction? Why these lines of an old song?

> Westron winde, when will thou blow,
> The smalle raine downe can raine?

An indefinable juxtaposition of words. Something with an undefinable life of its own will perhaps hint at the elusive meaning I mentioned earlier. W. B. Yeats says in 'The Symbolism of Poetry': 'All sounds, all colours, all forms, either because of their pre-ordained energies or because of long association, evoke indefinable yet precise emotions.' An image will call forth this response when it has some mirror of the emotion within itself, or when it has a power of its own.

The images in T. S. Eliot's 'Marina' provoke in me a feeling of quiet and a sharp yet calm sense of loss. I think Yeats has gone some way towards answering my question when he puts this power down to pre-ordained energies or long association. Perhaps these two things are closely bound together. The long association could cause the energy. But there is more to it than this. Samuel Beckett said that it is impossible to use English without writing poetry, and that the associations of the words may obscure the meaning, so that he preferred to write in French. One word may have its general, complex meanings, evolved through its history, and also a particular meaning for you, yourself. In the line from 'Marina'

> What sea what shores what granite islands towards my
>     timbers

the word 'granite' contains the qualities of granite (hardness, strength, impenetrability, resistance to time); the texture (rough and flinty); the colour (grey, with white flecks). For me it conjures up memories of childhood holidays in Cornwall, with great stones on Bodmin Moor and grey granite houses in villages round Land's End.

The image the word gives me is not necessarily the same as Eliot's image. Our experience of granite is bound to differ because we are different people, have lived different lives, and react to things in different ways. The image, made of words, gives something different, says something different, to everyone who reads the poem. 'Granite island' is not what I see and feel when I read the words, nor is it what anyone else sees and feels – not even the poet who wrote it. It is a synthesis of all these things. Like Eliot's Chinese jar in 'Burnt Norton', it

> Moves perpetually in its stillness.

It has some identity of its own that lingers and works in the imagination. I may think I have caught it by putting it down on paper; but it soars out of my hands. If this were not so, I doubt whether poetry would be of much value to anyone but the person who wrote it.

The image acts as a catalyst on the idea or feeling as it was when the poet conceived it and as it becomes in the mind of the reader when he interprets it. It cannot show the same truth to everyone who reads the poem, but it provides glimpses of a central truth.

The poet rarely thinks of the reader's reactions; and the reader, though he may want to know what the poet meant, seldom thinks that he must reproduce his creative feeling. Yet both play their parts in the image – the reader deepening the life that the poet gives it. This was brought home to me in an English seminar. I read the rest of the group a poem I had written about a transient love. I feared that so personal an emotion might embarrass the listeners. But some of them said that they had experienced this feeling themselves, so that the poem had relevance for them. I realized that it had ceased to be my poem. They had made it their own, substituting their experience for mine. I, by writing, had given them this particular experience at that time and place, even if I had, in a sense, lost the poem. It had taken on new aspects, new lives, which I had never created.

I have tried to show that an image may have a life of its own, independent of its maker. Once the poet has breathed life into it, like the new-born child it can breathe for itself.

## 3
### *The structure of the image*

An image is a relationship between thought (the truth or meaning that the poet wants to express), feeling (the tone of the poem and also the emotion in the reader, which matches it), and form (the words, which have properties such as rhythm). In weak images the parts are imperfectly fused.

The clearest way to investigate this three-fold structure is to take a single image. In Cleopatra's speech over Antony's body, the first image is the cry

The crown o' the earth doth melt.

Shakespeare has emotion in the grandeur of the image and in the loaded word 'crown', which implies Antony's value and position. He has the thought of decay, and of sovereignty lost, of things being awry (crowns don't usually melt). We are to marvel that this can happen, and to regret it – as the word 'melt' shows us. Finally, these two, feeling and thought, are united in the words, which besides giving us the meaning (Antony's dying) and dictating the way we are to feel this, echo these things in their sounds and rhythms. 'The crown o' the earth' is a marvellous image because it has so many layers of meaning, and evocations. It also echoes the theme of the play, its words suggesting royalty and power and world-dealing on a grand scale.

Images in poetry are rarely isolated. Ezra Pound's canto which begins 'With usura . . .' builds up in images a picture of what happens when corruption reigns. The picture is seen from many angles:

With usura, sin against nature,
is thy bread ever more of stale rags
is thy bread dry as paper,
with no mountain wheat, no strong flour
with usura the line grows thick
with usura is no clear demarcation
and no man can find site for his building.
Stone cutter is kept from his stone
weaver is kept from his loom . . .

Each image is changed subtly by being in a relationship with another. Whatever meaning is given is not of one image or the other, but a combination of several.

I may have given the impression that an image is a mere component, having life only when it is part of a relationship. This is akin to what Keats says of the poet in a letter to Woodhouse: 'A Poet is the most unpoetical of any thing in existence: because he has no identity . . .'. If the poet has no identity, and assumes one only when the force of another's personality gives him its shadow to wear, then might this not be the case with the image? It assumes fresh depths according to its closeness to other images in the poem, and also according to its relationship with its readers, their personalities and experiences. Has it, then, no identity? Or has it a life when it is cut out of its context and forced to stand by itself? It is useful to remember that Keats also wrote (in a letter to his brother and sister-in-law), 'I do not live in this world alone but in a thousand worlds.' The image is richer and subtler because there is no end to the permutations it can be involved in, to the shades of meaning it can imply, and to the pictures it can evoke. Yet has it, even so, an identity of its own? Is it a structure in its own right? In human personality the answer would have to be yes, because the interaction between the strands which make it up would still be an individual one. In an image the answer will be the same if there is something there that lives and intrigues and is not satisfactorily explained by a mechanical dividing into strands. I think this is true of great images. The line from *Antony and Cleopatra* could not be explained entirely, because the complexity of its motifs defies analytical probing.

In the course of this essay the image, which began as a tool, a component of poetry, has become an existence in its own right: one that can defeat man, who tries to tame it.

4

## *Tradition and the image*

I have not yet asked the question, Why is it that imagery can exert so strong a hold over man? This implies a second question, For what purpose does an image work? Sean O'Casey in his play *Within the Gates* has an interchange which is relevant to this second question. The Atheist and the Dreamer are debating over possession of the girl's soul:

*Atheist*  Song? Oh, I had no time for song!
*Dreamer*  You led her from one darkness into another, man.
　　　　　Will none of you ever guess that man can study man,
　　　　　or worship God, in dance and song and story!

The Dreamer says that the art form may be man's way of communicating with things outside his knowledge and comprehension.

In *Autobiographies*, Yeats writes of the symbolic people in his poems—Michael Robartes, Owen Aherne, Red Hanrahan: 'Because those imaginary people are created out of the deepest instincts of man, to be his measure and his norm, whatever I can imagine those mouths speaking may be the nearest I can go to truth.' These people, themselves images, are what Yeats calls different masks of himself. They teach him something by releasing knowledge of which he is not aware. In 'The Phases of the Moon', Aherne and Robartes discuss the poet himself:

*Aherne*　　　　　　　　　　　Why should not you
　　　Who know it all ring at his door, and speak
　　　Just truth enough to know that his whole life
　　　Will scarcely find for him a broken crust

Of all those truths that are your daily bread;
And when you have spoken take the roads again?

It may be that a man like Yeats could face this truth only by finding it in the mouth of his opposite. Robartes, for instance, the scholar-visionary and recluse, unlike Yeats, had no other qualities that pulled him apart or confused his attitudes. This is Yeats using the image, that which embodies some other life, to search for truth hidden in his own life. He supports my view that it is the image that gives us truth, not the poet through the image.

It almost seems to me that a serious confrontation with a great image is a religious experience. Yeats asks, again in *Autobiographies*, 'Have not all races their first unity from a mythology, that marries them to rock and hill?' It seems to me that words, of all things, carry with them this marriage. They have grown with man through the ages; they retain his feeling for birth-right – in their meanings, or in sounds. Pound in his essay 'A Retrospect' says that the natural object is 'the proper and perfect symbol'. Is not an image most frequently the representation of a natural object? The language of rock and hill has found its way into the work of great poets, and predominates there; it goes back to man's half remembered past, when life was stable and natural.

In 'The Dry Salvages' Eliot is concerned with the void of modern life, a rootless world where spiritual values seem to be dead and in which there seems to be nothing to turn to for support. He revives his childhood memories of New England:

> The salt is on the briar rose,
The fog is in the fir trees.

Is this because these words are the only ones that can give an inkling of the vast meanings he is trying to communicate? Or is it because words and memories like these offer something to hold on to when all is 'drifting wreckage'?

Man today is many centuries younger than the image, which has a past and a present, memories, and feelings, all contained in it. In a world of soulless animation, he should be able to take comfort from it, draw strength from it.

### *Joy*

These paragraphs from a letter Joy sent me just before Easter 1966 give the context of her learning about the creative process; and, like the criticism of Klee's plant forms in her essay and the children's tree shapes in her village diary, they reflect a characteristic energy. The pieces of writing she mentions were short poems.

My mind has been vainly struggling to know and order the strange emotions that have been running amok inside me over the past few weeks. I'm ill-equipped for self-knowledge. Attempts tire me out, or lead me to despair. I wish, sometimes, that I could just live, and not know. The books I read lay great stress on self-knowledge, but I'm beginning to feel very critical of my own attempts. I seem to take experiences, and worry them until

I can extract them, hold them in my hand, and examine them objectively – know them and label them, and file them away carefully for further use. I'm not sure that I'm in a position to label. Maybe I put on the wrong labels, and misuse experiences. I'm beginning to think it's much better to live intuitively – to feel life.

This criticism of experiences takes place after the event. I've noticed that I seem to live two lives (not at the same time). Some of the time I'm uncritical and unthinkingly happy. These are the times that I like to think of as the most real. I seem to feel a close contact with my environment, and see a reflection of my own life in natural things around me. At these times, I'm capable of strong emotion; I feel strong in myself with a conviction that I'm alive.

Then for days and weeks, I seem to be coldly ruled by my mind. The world shrinks – I shrink. I can't see. I care for nothing, and I experience no emotions. I seem almost to forget who I am. Now I wonder, is this maturity? Are the periods of elation just a youthful characteristic – when the world seems promising and myself full of untapped potential – even, perhaps, just potential to live?

I'm thoroughly mixed up in the problem. I've come to mistrust both sides. Neither side can comprehend the other.

Those two pieces of writing I showed you – I wrote them when the two sides seemed to meet. They are the very poor products of what to me was a huge self-realization. They are so inadequate, when I think of what was inside me when I wrote them, that I shan't write anything in that form again.

I suppose I mistrust everything I think and do, and so I wouldn't presume again to attempt to write poems. There is a consolation, though. If the periods when I feel really alive are merely a characteristic of my youth, they are very exciting. I hope they continue, because I'm sure I shall never have the consolation of calm wisdom in their place. I'll never be a great thinker! I wish I was sure I had adequate potential just to live; but even that's a bit vague. I'm impatient. I long for the certainty of strong talent in some direction. I'm afraid of never achieving anything worth while. Success for most people is the result of hard work and patience. I'm not sure whether I can apply myself to this, even if I find the way. I'll never achieve anything unless it takes a seat at the back.

Joy's second subject was design. Like Vic, she was an outstandingly good potter.

In spite of her misgivings about her capacity for hard work and patience, she has concentrated in her long essay the reading and the thought for three separate studies: of a painter, a dancer, and a poet. She looks at these three men in relation to one another, finding resemblances within their differences that lead her to a central truth.

The essay goes back to her talk on Paul Klee in her first year. Later, a friend introduced her to Nijinsky's Diary. At the end of her second year, she wrote on Yeats's 'Byzantium'.

When she began to read for her essay, she had not known why Klee, Nijinsky, and Yeats had come together in her mind. At first she had wanted to include Beckett as a contrast; but when the link between the other three became clear, she decided against this.

Her section on Klee began as a collection of autobiographical details, quotations from his writings, and comments in the style of art critics and historians. She had not absorbed her reading into her experience. By working in the vacation she had saved enough money to go to Berne and look at the Klees there. We saw that, if it was to be of any value, she would have to make this part of her essay her own exploration of Klee's work, using her experience and her reading in the service of his meaning.

## The Creative Process

*A Study of the Work of Paul Klee, Vaslav Nijinsky, and W. B. Yeats*

### Introduction

I began thinking of the creative process two years ago, in connection with Paul Klee and Coleridge. The possibility of infinite creation fascinated me.

I knew that each of Klee's paintings was a crystallization from the unconscious that Livingston Lowes speaks of in *The Road to Xanadu*. I knew that this must be so; for how else could I be instinctively drawn to something that I did not consciously understand?

The purpose of this essay is to try to make articulate what at the moment is mainly intuitive. Over the last two years I have been relating the work of other artists to the little I know of the creative process in Klee and Coleridge. I have reached the conclusion that, no matter how individual their work may be, genuine artists create in the same way. If I come to understand the way in which Klee, Nijinsky, and Yeats create, then allowing for the individuality of character and medium, I will have a starting point from which I can approach the work of other artists. If I had believed that a study of each artist would be an end in itself, I would not have begun this essay in the first place.

### I

### Paul Klee

When I look at a painting or a drawing by Paul Klee, I feel that I am being shown something that I have always known but never been consciously aware of. This continually expands my awareness.

As in all Klee's work except for the very early, purely representational kind, the forms in *Ad Marginem* are ambiguous. They are like images in poetry. They merge and take shape, then shift to mean something quite different. The painting becomes many things while I look at it: a drop of stagnant water under a microscope; cells continually being attracted to a central nucleus; a perfect form crystallizing out of chaos; sun seen through a mist or through water. It suggests ever-changing organic growth, a growth I never see but can feel when I am in the country. Someone else's response to it will probably be different.

When *Ad Marginem* was painted, Klee had already discovered the way to express what he wanted to say. In 1902 he wrote in his diary,

'I want to be as new-born .... to be almost primitive. Then I want to do something very modest, to work out for myself a tiny motif, one that my pencil will be able to encompass without any technique.'

To become as though new-born is no easy thing to achieve. It took Klee ten years to evolve a style entirely his own. He didn't wish to cut himself off from all outside experiences and from other artists; but he knew how important it was not to copy others if he wished to find himself through his art. That is why he began tentatively with the minutest forms.

The Impressionists seem always to have been aware of the transience of life. Paintings like Monet's *Canal at Zaandam*, Camille Pissarro's *The Apple Pickers*, Manet's *A Bar at the Folies-Bergère*, are of an isolated moment, and speak only of that moment. I think these painters had the first glimpse of an orderless world. The reality that they could perceive through their senses points to the inner world that Klee explores. Once they have captured a moment from a sequence of ever-changing moments, it stays there for ever. Klee produces works that are ever-changing in themselves. It is a truism that the artist reflects man's response to the universe in his time. In speaking of the Impressionists, I have tried to show that man, at the turn of the century, saw himself as a chance happening in an orderless world.

The Dadaists felt that, taken out of context, most of the things round us are useless and laughable, so they mocked the reality we perceive through our senses. René Magritte's *Time Transfixed* is a painting of a train rushing through a fireplace. Most of the short-lived movements attempted to destroy in order to create. Klee started afresh to create another world, a world that had become obscure.

When art seemed to be coming to a full stop, painters and psychologists began to delve into the unconscious. Klee wrote in *Creative Confession*: '... the Impressionists were perfectly right to live with the trailing vines and underbrush of everyday appearances. But our pounding heart drives us down, deep down to the primordial underground.' The 'primordial underground' had been glimpsed by Bosch, Goya, Blake, and a few other isolated artists; never before had it been stressed in this way. Though outwardly it may have appeared that man was insecure in a purposeless world, Klee, looking into the meaning of our existence, saw all life shooting from common springs.

In his teaching at the Bauhaus he used materials that did not appear to have anything to do with painting: cloth, tin-foil, filings, glass. The students had to study these closely, describe their special properties, and then make suggestions for their use. They had to eliminate all thought of self-expression – as if all creation were a surprise. Klee calls this process 'finding a soul in insignificant things': 'The artist does not render the visible, rather he makes visible.' He aimed at 'Genesis eternal'. By seeking to penetrate, even to become, an object, he tried to understand what forces determine its qualities. The drawing for *Plants, Earth and Kingdom of the Air* illustrate this point. The forms in this drawing are not like any plants I have ever seen, yet I know they are plants. I feel that the earth is fertile and that these plants are rapidly growing. I can feel the sap rising. Klee studied vast quantities of plant life. His Notebooks are filled with minutely detailed drawings. The plants in this drawing look like the very earliest forms. They show me how plants grow. They are swelling, bursting, and flowering. This is the result of Klee's deep understanding of plants.

He writes in his *Pedagogical Sketchbook*:

'From the roots the sap rises up into the artist, flows through him, flows to his eyes. [By "sap" he means experience.] He is the trunk of the tree. Seized and moved by the force of the current, he directs his vision into his work . . . No one will expect a tree to form its crown in exactly the same way as its roots. The artist is accused of distortion – he transmits. And the beauty of the crown is not his own; it has merely passed through him.' Here Klee is saying that an artist cannot work in isolation. The life-giving force is experience. Without it there would be no flowering. The artist must see and feel the life in everything around him.

*Game on the Water* shows the life beneath the surface. This very simple pen and ink drawing could be taken to represent the graining on a piece of wood. The lines flow across the page, packed with energy. Each affects the lines around it; a bump in one changes the flow of the others. The lines are wavering, their forces ever changing. It is a drawing of the swirl of currents under what we see.

The Expressionist painters saw life behind the calm exterior, but what they saw seems to be a caricature. The world is heightened by the artists' unrest. Their work bears witness to a violence that comes from within themselves. Such paintings as Eduard Munch's *The Cry* say more about the men themselves than about anything else. If Klee's students had been concerned with self-expression, they would not have seen the individual life in 'insignificant things'.

He himself records chance observations and happenings, notes new techniques, and keeps a record of his son Felix's weight. His notebooks are like Leonardo da Vinci's, or Coleridge's. In theirs, too, nothing is unimportant or taken for granted; every aspect of their lives is relevant to their work: 'For the artist, communication with nature remains the most essential condition. The artist is human; himself part of nature . . .'

Klee and Coleridge seem to me to resemble one another in several ways. One evening in Tunisia Klee wrote in his Diary: 'Many a blond, northern moonrise, like a muted reflection, will softly remind me again and again. It will be my bride, my alter ego. An incentive to find myself. I myself am the moonrise of the South.' In this statement his experience is so acute that it emerges in a poetical form. It is perhaps one of the most important experiences of his life: he had understood what it meant to enter into an object in a union so close that he compares it to a betrothal. I think this is the conscious realization of the deep feeling he had in 1900 when he declared, 'I am God.' The conscious perception of an experience has led to a deeper intuition which I can feel rather than explain when I look at his paintings. Everything seems to be inevitable. In *Fragment from a Ballet for Aeolian Harp*, filament-like transparencies of soft colour are wafted to the cadences of the harp. The figures flow and dissolve in the music. Coleridge, too, assimilates experiences in this way. An extract from one of his notebooks describes his children playing. They are 'a miniature of the agitated trees'. The trees and the children combine in an exultant dance of life: the experience becomes an image. This happens when there is a fusion of acute sensitivity, intuition, and intellect.

Coleridge says in chapter vi of *Biographia Literaria* that when the mind is passive it is the slave of outward impressions and senseless memory; and Klee realized that if he expected the process of assimilation to happen unconsciously, he would produce nothing. In his tree analogy he is not saying that the crown of the tree is a re-assembled product of what was shaped at the root. The artist's conscious participation in experience is all-important. This participation is not merely intellectual; intellect is fused with intuition.

So far I have dealt with Klee's work on a superficial level; I have not attempted to interpret his symbolic painting. His paintings are themselves images – images of particular objects, or of more general significance. He believed that in every manifestation of nature there was a reflection of the whole, and that the contemplation of natural forms led to conclusions about the whole. He became as 'new-born' so that he could assimilate such experience freshly.

In their early work both Klee and Nijinsky feel the spirit of whatever they are expressing. Klee's paintings are conceived and interpreted through feeling. But they are not all feeling. The symbols that occur in his later work, coupled with his experiments in line, tone, and colour are worked out almost mathematically – though there is always evidence that he was led on by feeling. In his portrait of his wife Lily he doesn't try to make her beautiful. He shows her tenderness and her day-dreaming, yet there is a strength in her firm, tight mouth that goes beneath the impression of softness. There is an intelligent calculating mind behind the day-dreaming. This is my literal interpretation of his figurative technique. Line, colour, and tone take over; and they are inseparably linked with the idea. The picture gradually crystallizes into self-contained images.

Klee became aware that particular signs were drifting through his mind. Three of these – the pine, the moon, and the star – can be seen in *The Niesen*, a colour image of an African evening following an intensely hot day. Like Yeats, he recognized the importance of these recurring symbols. After studying his work, and that of Yeats and Nijinsky, I have come to think that symbols occur naturally in the truly creative minds: they occur because the artist has a glimpse of spiritual realities; and they are the only link between those realities and the realities of this world, which Yeats in *Autobiographies* calls the world of vegetation. Klee said in the *Pedagogical Sketchbook* that symbols brought comfort to his mind 'by making it realize that it is not confined to earthly potentialities'.

He understood that the medium of expression must be as subtle as the symbols and images to be expressed. Like Nijinsky's, his medium is as original as the feeling that necessitates its invention. In Nijinsky's choreography a movement of the body corresponds to a phrase in the music, and both are closely related to the idea that the dance expresses. In his essay 'Thoughts on Drawing and on Art in General', Klee describes 'the energy of the line, surface, and space' in terms of an imaginary walk: across a ploughed field (a flat surface marked with lines); basket weavers come home with their carts (a wheel); a flash of lightning on the horizon (a zig-zag line); late stars (a field of points).

It seems that to produce original works of art embodying the essence of his beliefs the artist must work out an entirely suitable medium. Once he has done this the process of creation is simple and natural. Both Nijinsky and Klee used sophisticated techniques, the result of hard work undertaken to achieve modes of expression that in primitive people and children are effortless. Some of my friends have responded to a painting of Klee's with the remark, 'It looks like the work of a five year old.' The difference is that the work of a five year old has not been fused with an idea, so it is questionable whether it is a work of art. *With Green Stockings* is much more than a picture of a girl's complete absorption in the movement of a ball. The ball is heavy. The girl's concentration makes her forget that she is about to catch it; and her arms are erect in the air while she is contemplating the absorbing mystery of the ball and its movement. Klee wishes to show her child-like characteristics, and so he uses his medium in what, looked at superficially, is a child-like way.

Towards the end of his life, his paintings became more symbolic. It is interesting to compare his drawings for *Plants, Earth and the Kingdom of the Air* with *The Park at Albien*, which was painted about nineteen years later. The forms no longer resemble plant forms, but are symbols of compact energy. They are like clenched fists: held in closed tension, they will release the full force of their energy at any moment. The only figurative parallel I could give is that of bracken fronds when they first push up through the ground; they, too, hold their energy like clenched fists. In the drawing I see the sap rise and the roots push through the ground; but my impression of growth is strictly confined to that of plants. The energy in *The Park at Albien* is the energy of all nature. It is the energy of the mushroom that can force its way through concrete. It is the energy innate in all matter. Through his use of the symbol, Klee has led me in this painting to more profound feeling.

In his last work, he tends more and more to abstraction. The symbols dominate and speak in a way that defies explanation. If an explanation is possible, I am in no way provided to give it. All I can say is that I find such works as *Towards Right, Towards Left*, and *Red Waistcoat* moving, and often exciting.

Klee created a lost world in a new form. The lost world is the world where symbols had a fresh and vital meaning, and men lived by them. A symbol may live unchanged even though it is forgotten or ignored; it stays deeply embedded in man's subconscious mind. Paul Klee felt that its rejuvenation would perhaps lift man from the soul-destroying material life and re-connect him with the 'latent realities' which exist in this world. The symbol is the only link between man's spiritual and material lives. By opening the door to a world which has no limits and whose manifestations in this world are also limitless, he showed that infinite creation is possible. The value of the plastic arts cannot be over-estimated; he showed that they are capable of expressing the whole of life.

Nijinsky reached what I think must have been perfection at more or less the same time that Klee evolved the basis for his creative work. I have tried to show the similarity between the two – a similarity which I hope to make clearer as I study the way in which Nijinsky created.

## 2

## *Vaslav Nijinsky*

Klee said, 'The artist is human; himself part of nature...'; and Nijinsky wrote in his Diary, 'Nature is life.... I understand it because I feel it and Nature feels me.... But I study it only through feeling.' Nijinsky had mastered his technique completely, but in everything else he was spontaneous: 'Whenever I have a feeling, I carry it out. I never fight against feeling.' In Klee's art, intellect was always important. I think the difference between them is partly the result of the different demands made by their media.

Thinking about this difference has led me to ask the question, Is dance the purest and most direct medium of expression? I hope I shall be able to answer this after studying the life and art of Nijinsky, whom the French called 'le Dieu de la Dance'.

His wife shows in her biography that he had lived ballet from the age of three, accustomed to parents 'who suddenly became knights and princesses, nymphs and fauns', so that he 'could not distinguish between reality and fairy-tale'. Technique, which he had mastered at sixteen, was not enough to satisfy him; Alexander Benois (in *Reminiscences of the Russian Ballet*) describes him as he danced *Le Pavilion d'Armide*: 'Having put on the costume, he gradually began to change into another being ... He became re-incarnated and actually entered into the next existence.' Later he himself wrote in his Diary, 'I am all life, infinity. I will be always and everywhere.' In an essay printed in the Catalogue to the 1954 exhibition Tamara Karsavina says of Diaghilev that he believed that art 'must develop as a living organism, finding in the process of its growth new modes of expression to translate the new thoughts, the new discoveries of the human intellect.' Nijinsky was allowed free expression in all his roles.

Frank Kermode writes in *The Romantic Image*: 'The language of the freely-moving dancer is more like the Image than the virtuosity of the ballerina's more limited range of movement.' Nijinsky wanted his dancing to express truths through images. In *Spectre de la Rose*, where he seems to have taken classical dance to its limits, his famous leap defying gravity symbolized for many people the aspirations of the soul towards God. He told his wife that he wished to express 'love in its divine sense'.

In 1911 he began to make *L'Après-midi d'un Faune*, a ballet that would retain its unity even if it were danced without music. He took for his theme the awakening of emotions and the sexual instincts. This theme could be an analogy to his own creative awakening: I think the story is a symbolic expression of his intentions as an artist. He set it in ancient Greece, which he associated with the adolescence of art. He cut movement to an essential – as a poet or painter would choose the minimum of words or signs to convey an image; and sculpted the dancers as if they were clay. He told Diaghilev, 'I have in mind a choreographic poem.' He wanted to plant seeds in the minds of the audience that would continue to grow long after they had left the theatre. His 'poem' has an overall idea that is expressed in a series of images. The idea links the parts together, and the whole can be interpreted on different levels.

In *Le Sacre du Printemps*, he drew, like Klee, on primitive sources. The artist who understands 'the divine life' manifest in any period may find that his understanding will develop into creation, and that this creation will take a form that is essentially of his own time. It may also contain the seeds of the period that has inspired it. Both *Le Sacre du Printemps* and *L'Après-midi d'un Faune* are illustrations of Yeats's remark in his essay on 'The Symbolism of Poetry' that inspiration comes to artists in 'beautiful and startling shapes' because '. . . the divine wars upon our outer life, and must needs change its weapons and its movements as we change ours'.

The dancers' movements in *Le Sacre du Printemps* express fear, joy, ecstasy. God, in this case a primitive god, gives and takes all. The music reflects the rhythm of life that flows through us and links us with the earth. Later in his essay, Yeats asks, 'How can the arts overcome the slow dying of men's hearts that we call the progress of the world . . . without becoming the garments of religion. . . ?'

Yeats, Klee, and Nijinsky all wished to serve mankind through their art. They each returned to the symbol which has meaning for all men and can express eternal truths.

In his last dance Nijinsky was the embodiment of an image that for Yeats symbolized pure creation. Yeats's image was of a dancing woman with a perfect body, described by Frank Kermode: '. . . the face without intellectual disturbance, the meaning fully incarnate, no obtrusive "character", for as long as the dance lasts the dancer cannot be distinguished from it.' That Nijinsky was a man does not detract from his fulfilment of this image: the essence of the image being that the dancer symbolizes perfect beauty which cannot be embodied in this life. Had Yeats seen Nijinsky dance, I think he would have agreed that he came as close as it is possible to come to the embodiment of the image.

Romola Nijinsky describes how in the Suvretta at St. Moritz in January 1918 he danced 'the war, with its suffering, with its destruction, with its death': the war, he told his audience, 'which you did not prevent and so . . . are also responsible for'. He would show them, he said, how artists live, suffer, and create. On his way to the Suvretta he said that it was the day of his marriage with God. Later that day he wrote in his Diary, 'I felt the presence of God the whole evening.'

In this last dance there were moments of perfect unity. The creation and the execution were one. Yeats called this unity thought rushing out to the edges of the flesh. While the dance lasted, Nijinsky was capable of creating and dancing anything.

After this he gradually lost touch with his former character. It is impossible for me to diagnose why, from my limited knowledge of his earlier life; or to say whether it was inevitable; or to relate his insanity to his genius. The cause may have been what Yeats called 'the cost of the image'. Perhaps Nijinsky's insight was too much for him to bear. If he had not gone mad at this point, I wonder how long he would have been able to dance away the sins of the world.

Nijinsky did for dance what Klee did for painting. They both went back to the beginning of our experience, and revitalized the symbols. Klee showed us the symbols themselves, the arrow and the circle; or pointed to them in images. Nijinsky in his dancing *became* the symbol, and created it before the eyes of the audience. Yeats says in his essay how hard it is to 'give a body to something that moves beyond the senses'. Nijinsky succeeded in giving a body to the spiritual life; and like the dancer that recurs as an image in Yeats's poems, he achieved moments of perfection.

## 3
## *W. B. Yeats*

> I have no speech but symbol, the pagan speech I made
> Amid the dreams of youth.
>
> *Upon a Dying Lady*

Yeats, like Klee and Nijinsky, rediscovered the symbol. Just as they had connected their arts with the main stream of life, he revitalized the art of poetry. I think that these three may be the most important artists of the century. As far as I have been able to discover, they never met. It is no coincidence that they all turned to the symbol at more or less the same time. All three are concerned about society's growing preoccupation with the material world. The artist is perhaps the only person capable of sensing the needs of a society.

Of the three, Yeats delved most deeply into the meanings and associations of symbols. In the poem quoted at the beginning of this section, he says that throughout his life they are the one constant element in his work.

His poem 'Byzantium' has many meanings. Richard Ellmann in *W. B. Yeats, the Man and the Mask* sees it primarily as a description of the act of making a poem. I think it could represent the whole act of creation. I choose to discuss it because I believe that in it Yeats is saying, 'This is how a work of art comes into being.' In Yeats the act of creation was always a self-conscious one. He tried like Klee to understand everything that was happening in his mind, even the images that appeared there. He could perhaps be described as shaping an experience while it was in process of becoming a part of him.

The sea, which is an image of the chaos of the world, and also, in this poem, of imagination, wells up to the marble dancing floor of Byzantium. In Yeats's mind, the city was an image of perfect unity of being, and of eternity. It was eternally beautiful because of this unity. He looked back to the Byzantine age as a time when thought and action were one. In *A Vision* he speaks of the eyes of Byzantine statues: they are holes drilled in ivory. He saw these eyes staring out into eternity, beyond the action of the moment. The statues embody some of the qualities in that other image for unity of being, the dancing woman with the expressionless face.

Images are born of imagination – 'That dolphin-torn, that gong-tormented sea' – and the smithies that break the flood are the smithies of the intellect. Creation arises when the two, imagination and intellect, come together.

In 'Among School Children', Yeats speaks of the act of creation in what must be its ideal form:

Labour is blossoming or dancing where
The body is not bruised to pleasure soul,
Nor beauty born out of its own despair,
Nor blear eyed – wisdom out of midnight oil.
O chestnut tree, great rooted blossomer,
Are you the leaf, the blossom or the bole?
O body swayed to music, O brightening glance,
How can we know the dancer from the dance?

This ease in creation could not be achieved until Yeats had mastered the symbols and images which were part of his vocabulary as an Irish poet. Both he and Klee used the tree as a symbol of self-contained, effortless creation. I have spoken of Klee's conscious analysis of his experience. Yeats's tree is 'great rooted': he believed that experience is drawn from a broad area. His poetry did not come without a great deal of intellectual preoccupation with the experience at the root of the tree. The symbol of the tree stresses the unity of a work of art; I couldn't look at the blossoms without connecting them with the leaves or the roots.

In this extract from 'Among School Children' I think Yeats has in mind another kind of unity as well, a unity that you can see only by looking into what is near to you: your village, the cobweb on your walls. *A Vision*, thirty years later, is a development of this early thought. Yeats believed, not that points of perfection could exist only in a spiritual world, but that spiritual life where perfection is possible was, like the blossom of the tree, part of this world and manifest in it.

Though he and Paul Klee examined symbols analytically, they always retained their belief in the ultimate mystery that had not been solved by Darwin. Nijinsky longed for men to live in a way that was too perfect for them. Klee found a soul in 'insignificant' things, and Yeats looked back to a time when men's actions were significant and creative: significant because the universe had meaning – down to the smallest grass-blade, which was symbolic of the whole. Today our environment has lost much of its meaning, and is related to us on a utilitarian basis.

From this material world Yeats turned, in the poems written between 1893 and 1899, to the symbol of the rose. In the preface to *Letters to the New Island*, quoted by A. G. Stocks (in *W. B. Yeats, History and Thought*), he looks back on these poems: 'My isolation from ordinary men and women was increased by an aestheticism destructive of mind and body, combined with an adoration of physical beauty that made it meaningless.' I think he is being too harshly self-critical here. The poems are like echoes from another world and time; they come from the heart of his isolation, an isolation that was essential to their writing. I think he was impatient with them because they expressed emotion not shaped by intellect. It is perhaps for this reason that I find it hard to understand anything more than that I have felt an emotional response. In 'The Symbolism of Poetry' he says:

'It is the intellect that decides where the reader shall ponder over the procession of the symbols, and if the symbols are merely emotional, he gazes from amid the accidents and destinies of the world; but if the symbols are intellectual too, he becomes himself a part of pure intellect, and is himself mingled with the procession.'

The poet's task is to shape the symbols intellectually and, through their contrasts and associations, lead the reader to the idea or mood of the poem. I think Yeats's early work would suffer if a reader attempted an intellectual explanation.

From 1900 onwards his poems underwent a drastic change. Their detachment is different from the isolation of the earlier poems. Many of them are spoken in dialogue, or sound as though they are the words of a second person: he let his ideas develop through someone else's character. The other characters suggest different facets of the idea, so that he has a much wider field in which to work. This detachment is important because the artist does not speak for himself alone, but for all men. He wrote in a letter to Sean O'Casey: 'A dramatist can help his characters to educate him by thinking and studying everything that gives them the language they are groping for through his hands and eyes, but the control must be theirs.' In this way, the artist is always learning, and never runs the risk of being opinionated. There is always someone to speak for him. I think this is why the dancing woman wears a mask: she is the medium of the idea, which is the dance.

Yet it is the artist who is creating and being developed—through continuous activity and over a long period of time. Spontaneous creation is a very rare thing, possible only among primitive peoples and a few isolated individuals. Our feelings may be basically the same as those of primitive man; but they can be embodied only in forms that are made by the use of intellectual techniques, and these are complex. Primitive simplicity is no longer natural to man; it is natural only in children.

In *A Vision*, human passions and complexities are important as parts of the whole of experience. The soul, or 'diamon', doesn't discard experience, but distils and purifies it into an irreducible essence. In the same way, the symbol is a distillation of man's passions accumulated round an object. It contains in itself all the aspects of a particular experience, and is related to the whole. It becomes a norm of experience and so, eternal; remaining in its perfect form as a link between this world and the world of spiritual essences. It stands above the world of the diamons because they are still part of human complexities, striving towards eternal perfection.

Byzantium, in Yeats's mind, became such a symbol of perfection: it was the one period of history when an idea had been embodied in a civilization. I think that it could also represent the poet himself. When a poem is created, the images, rising from the turmoil of the unconscious, are shaped by intellect. Yeats is able to create because the archetypes are known to him. It is impossible to tell to what extent this is a conscious process. He says in 'The Symbolism of Poetry' that at the moment of creation he is both asleep and awake. The rhythm of the poem, 'hushing us with an alluring monotony', keeps us awake by variety: a state in which the mind, 'liberated from the pressure of the will, is unfolded in symbols'.

I imagine that creation did not come as easily as this when he first began to write. He had to work to make his language transparent to his thoughts. In the state of trance described in this quotation his thoughts, and the language of images and symbols which spoke the thoughts, seem to be created at the same moment. It is impossible to say which came first, thought or image: 'How can we know the dancer from the dance?'

In its moments of perfection, the image strives to assume an eternal form. The spirits, or images, come to the marble dancing floor of Byzantium. They are moulded in the smithies of the intellect, then once more cast out into the world. This is a continual process, because these images 'fresh images beget'. Creation is an eternal and limitless process.

'Byzantium' could be interpreted as representing eternal creation either of man or of the image. I think the two are inseparable.

The creative process in Yeats, Klee, and Nijinsky is an analogy to the creation of all men and the universe. I believe that an artist reaches moments of perfection when his intellect and the spiritual power within him, which forces him to create, achieve what Yeats called 'unity of being'. When I look at a painting by Klee, or read one of Yeats's poems, I can perhaps sense or imagine this moment of unity, and understand why Klee could say, 'I am God', and Yeats, 'I am a crowd'. They show me that eternity and unity are embodied in this world. But they can never give me the perfection of that moment of creation. Paintings and words can grow in my mind; but these experiences are always, in a sense, second-hand. I never saw Nijinsky dance; but I imagine that to see him 'dance the war' would have made me part of his experience while his dance was being created. He must have been, like the dancer in 'Byzantium', dancing in flames. I think only a dancer could involve me in so direct a way.

Artists have to reach out to the spiritual world with media that are necessarily of this world. Klee, Yeats, and Nijinsky did not point towards a spiritual abstraction, but saw that the spiritual is here and now. I believe that this was their only possible way of showing that there is such a thing as spiritual life and mystery. Their work is full of hope, because they knew that there was still a great mystery behind existence, that each man is part of this mystery, and that all are linked with one another, with all past generations and with the universe. They allow for the diversity of man, and see that infinite creation is possible. The universe does not operate as a closed system; it is a fluid, organic whole; and each manifestation, down to the blade of grass, is a reflection or aspect of what could be called God, or preferably, I think, the mystery. The hope of the painter, the dancer, and the poet is shown in their turning to the symbol and their seeing in it a link between the temporal and the spiritual worlds.

These paragraphs from a diary were written in October 1964. At the beginning of their course, the students spend a month in village schools, in Somerset, Gloucestershire, or Wiltshire. I kept a copy of these two entries, and found it recently in a bundle of school practice notes. I was struck by Joy's awareness: the life in her responding to the life in the children, responding to the living plants:

The children's trees are so much more lively and varied than my own.

They forgot that it was a tree that they were cutting out, and became intent on weaving in and out of the intricate spaces between the twigs. The shapes are full of movement. In some, the branches are like taut fingers and clawing hands. The trunk is like a pent up stream of energy that explodes at the top into zig-zag shapes.

(Some children had pressed flowers picked on their walk with Joy.)

David seemed to be especially sensitive to the fact that the plants had been crushed and flattened. He had chosen the most brilliant and perfect plants and flowers. Among them was a late rose that we had found growing in the corner of the field. When he saw the rose flattened and brown, he was unhappy, and asked me why I had killed it.

# References

Sources referred to in the text include:

KENNETH CLARK. *Landscape in Art* John Murray.

A. B. CLEGG. *The Excitement of Writing* Chatto and Windus.

KATHLEEN COBURN. *Inquiring Spirit* Routledge & Kegan Paul.

EMILY DICKINSON. *Selected Poems* edited by James Reeves, Heinemann.

HELEN GARDNER. *The Elegies and the Songs and Sonnets of John Donne* Oxford University Press.

ALAN GARNER. *The Weirdstone of Brisingamen* Penguin (Puffin).

ROBERT GITTINGS. *John Keats* Heinemann.

GUSTAV GLUCK. *Das Breughelbuch* Anton Schroll, Vienna.

WILLIAM GOLDING. *Lord of the Flies* Faber & Faber.

RENE GROUSSET. *L'Art de L'Extrême Orient* Librairie Plon, Paris.

THOMAS HARDY. *Far from the Madding Crowd* Macmillan.

J. LIVINGSTONE LOWES. *The Road to Xanadu* Vintage Books, New York.

SYBIL MARSHALL. *An Experiment in Education* Cambridge University Press.

ANDREW MARVELL. *Poems and Letters* edited by H. M. Margoliouth, Oxford University Press.

R. MONCKTON MILNES. *The Life and Letters of John Keats* J. M. Dent.

J. PORCHIER. *Les Très Riches Heures du Duc de Berry* Editions Nomis, Paris.

THE TIMES. obituary of C. T. R. Wilson.

J. R. R. TOLKIEN. *The Lord of the Rings* Allen and Unwin.

WORDSWORTH. *Poetical Works* edited by T. Hutchinson, Oxford University Press.

# Acknowledgements

The author and publishers wish to thank the National Gallery for permission to reproduce the detail from *The Annunciation* by Crivelli; the Pierpoint Morgan Library, New York, for permission to reproduce the portrait of Milton at the age of ten; Robin Tanner for permission to print entries from Edward Thomas's unpublished Notebook; Sir Kenneth Clark for permission to use material from his talk on symbols and images; the University of Cambridge for permission to quote from Alfred Wallis's letter; and students and children for their writing.

For permission to reprint copyright material, the author and publishers wish to thank:

George Allen and Unwin Ltd for extracts from 'The Hoard' taken from *The Adventures of Tom Bombadil, Tree and Leaf* by J. R. R. Tolkien;

The Bodley Head Ltd for an extract from *Poetry and Experience* by Archibald MacLeish;

Cambridge University Press Ltd for an extract from *Leonardo da Vinci* by Sir Kenneth Clark;

Jonathan Cape Ltd for an extract from Nijinsky's *Diary*;

The Clarendon Press Ltd for extracts from: *The Life of J. M. W. Turner* by A. J. Finberg, the preface to the *Oxford English Dictionary*, and *Collected Letters* of Samuel Taylor Coleridge edited by E. L. Griggs;

Chatto and Windus Ltd for an extract from *Memoirs* by Alexandre Benois (*Reminiscences of the Russian Ballet*), translated by Moura Budberg

J. M. Dent Ltd for extracts from *A Passage to India* by E. M. Forster;

Faber and Faber Ltd for extracts from: *Collected Shorter Poems, Cantos*, and *Literary Essays* by Ezra Pound, *Collected Poems 1909–1962* and *Selected Essays* by T. S. Eliot, *For the Union Dead* by Robert Lowell, *On Receiving the first Aspen Award* by Benjamin Britten, *Collected Poems* by Edwin Muir, *Collected Poems* by Stephen Spender, and *Selected Poems* by Wallace Stevens;

Eric Glass Ltd for an extract from *Nijinsky* by Romola Nijinsky;

Rupert Hart-Davis Ltd for an extract from *Coleridge* by Humphrey House, and for passages from W. B. Yeats, *Letters*, edited by Allan Wade;

The Hogarth Press Ltd for 'In the House of the Soul' from *The Complete Poems of C. P. Cavafy*, translated by Rae Dalven;

Lund Humphries Ltd for an extract from Paul Klee, *Notebooks, The Thinking Eye*, Volume 1 edited by Jurg Spiller;

Alfred Knopf Inc. for an extract from *Kings, Lords and Commons* by Frank O'Connor;

MacGibbon and Kee for an extract from *Sean O'Casey* by David Krause;

Macmillan & Co Ltd and the Trustees of the Hardy Estate for an extract from *Tess of the D'Urbervilles* by Thomas Hardy;

Mrs O'Casey and Macmillan & Co Ltd for an extract from *Within the Gates* from *Collected Plays II* by Sean O'Casey;

Daily Mirror Newspapers Ltd for 'Tom O'Bedlam' by Caroline Lois Matcham;

The Nonesuch Press Ltd for extracts from *Selected Essays* by Hazlitt, and from *Poetry and Prose* by William Blake, both edited by Sir Geoffrey Keynes;

Oxford University Press Ltd for extracts from: *Journals and Papers* by Gerard Manley Hopkins; *Memoirs* by Eleanor Farjeon; *Letters of John Keats* edited by M. Buxton Forman; *Poetry and Selected Prose of Henry Vaughan*; and *The Poems of Samuel Taylor Coleridge,* Edited by E. H. Coleridge;

Peter Owen Ltd for an extract from *Diaries* by Paul Klee, edited by Felix Klee;

Penguin Books Ltd for an extract by Wei T'ai from *Poems of the Late T'Ang* translated by A. C. Graham; and for a passage from *The Waning of the Middle Ages* by J. Huizinga;

Laurence Pollinger Ltd for an extract from 'Iris by Night' by Robert Frost, from *The Complete Poems of Robert Frost*, published by Jonathan Cape Ltd; and for 'Whatever man makes' from *The Complete Poems of D. H. Lawrence*, published by William Heinemann Ltd;

Routledge and Kegan Paul Ltd and the Bollingen Foundation, Princeton U. P. for extracts from *The Notebooks of Samuel Taylor Coleridge I* edited by Kathleen Coburn;

The Chilmark Press for an extract from *The Romantic Image* by Frank Kermode;

Martin Secker & Warburg Ltd for an extract from *The Wild Garden* by Angus Wilson;

A. P. Watt and Son, Mr M. B. Yeats and Macmillan & Co Ltd for extracts from the following poems by W. B. Yeats: 'The Wild Swans at Coole', 'The Wanderings of Oisin', 'Upon a Dying Lady', 'To a Child Dancing in the Wind', 'Among School Children', 'Byzantium', 'Coole and Ballylee 1931', 'The Phases of the Moon', 'The Double Vision of Michael Robartes', all taken from *Collected Poems*; also for extracts from *Autobiographies* (edited by Allan Wade), and *Essays and Introductions* by W. B. Yeats;

Leonard Woolf and The Hogarth Press Ltd for extracts from the novels of Virginia Woolf.

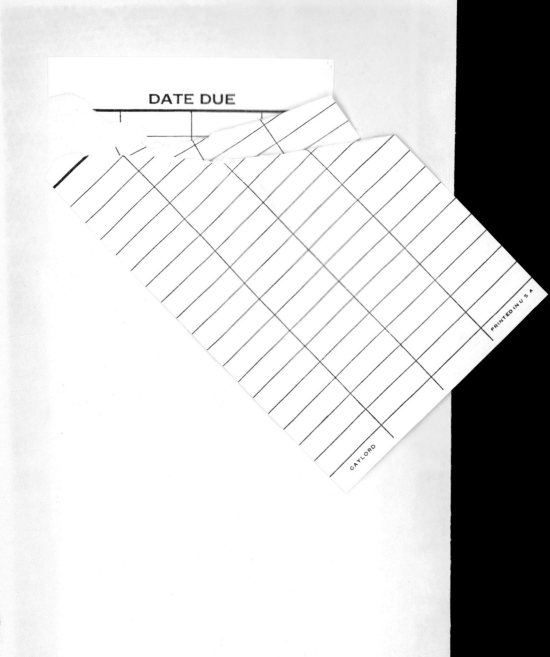

DATE DUE

GAYLORD

PRINTED IN U S A